Investigating the n
of Rotherhithe

Excavations at Pacific Wharf,

165 Rotherhithe Street, Southwark

MoLAS Archaeology Studies Series

1 A 14th-century pottery site in Kingston upon Thames, Surrey: excavations at 70–76 Eden Street, Pat Miller and Roy Stephenson
ISBN 1 901992 07 1

2 Excavations at 72–75 Cheapside/83–93 Queen Street, City of London, Julian Hill and Aidan Woodger
ISBN 1 901992 08 X

3 Bankside: excavations at Benbow House, Southwark, London SE1, Anthony Mackinder and Simon Blatherwick
ISBN 1 901992 12 8

4 A Romano-British cemetery on Watling Street: excavations at 165 Great Dover Street, Southwark, London, Anthony Mackinder
ISBN 1 901992 11 X

5 Excavations at 25 Cannon Street, City of London: from the Middle Bronze Age to the Great Fire, Nicholas J Elsden
ISBN 1 901992 22 5

6 The London Millennium Bridge: excavation of the medieval and later waterfronts at Peter's Hill, City of London, and Bankside, Southwark, Julian Ayre and Robin Wroe-Brown
ISBN 1 901992 25 X

7 An excavation in the western cemetery of Roman London: Atlantic House, City of London, Sadie Watson
ISBN 1 901992 26 8

8 The Roman tower at Shadwell, London: a reappraisal, David Lakin, with Fiona Seeley, Joanna Bird, Kevin Rielly and Charlotte Ainsley
ISBN 1 901992 27 6

9 Early modern industry and settlement: excavations at George Street, Richmond, and High Street, Mortlake, in the London Borough of Richmond upon Thames, Barney Sloane and Stewart Hoad, with John Cloake, Jacqueline Pearce and Roy Stephenson
ISBN 1 901992 35 7

10 Roman burials, medieval tenements and suburban growth: 201 Bishopsgate, City of London, Dan Swift
ISBN 1 901992 41 1

11 Investigating the maritime history of Rotherhithe: excavations at Pacific Wharf, 165 Rotherhithe Street, Southwark, Kieron Heard with Damian Goodburn
ISBN 1 901992 40 3

Investigating the maritime history of Rotherhithe

Excavations at Pacific Wharf, 165 Rotherhithe Street, Southwark

Kieron Heard with Damian Goodburn

MoLAS Archaeology Studies Series 11

Museum of London Archaeology Service

Published by the Museum of London Archaeology Service
Copyright © Museum of London 2003

A CIP catalogue record for this book is available from the British Library

Production and series design by Tracy Wellman
Typesetting and design by Susan Banks
Reprographics by Andy Chopping
Copy editing by Katherine Barclay
Series editing by Sue Hirst/Susan M Wright

Printed by the Lavenham Press

Front cover: view of the new building at Pacific Wharf, Rotherhithe; Frechen
stoneware drinking jug decorated with a medallion featuring the profile of a
possible Landsknecht soldier [63]; a Thames-side shipyard in 1843; one of the
trestles forming the foundation of Building 6

CONTRIBUTORS

Principal author	Kieron Heard
Woodworking evidence	Damian Goodburn
Post-medieval pottery	Nigel Jeffries
Clay tobacco pipes	Kieron Heard
Tree-ring analysis	Ian Tyers
Graphics	Helen Jones
Photography	Margaret Cox and Kieron Heard (site), Andy Chopping (pottery)
Project managers	Derek Seeley, Elizabeth Howe, Gordon Malcolm, Peter Rowsome
Editor	David Bowsher

CONTENTS

List of figures viii

Foreword ix

Summary x

Acknowledgements xi

Introduction   **1**

1.1   Location and circumstances of fieldwork 1

1.2   Historical background 3

Origins of the settlement at Rotherhithe 3

Medieval land reclamation 3

Origins of shipbuilding at Rotherhithe 4

Expansion of maritime industries in the 17th and
18th centuries 4

Decline of shipbuilding in the 19th century 4

1.3   Organisation of this report 5

1.4   Textual and graphical conventions in this report . . . 5

The archaeological sequence   **2**

2.1   Geology and topography (period 1) 6

The natural landscape (OA1) 6

Period 1: discussion 7

2.2   A probable timber yard, c 1650–1700 (period 2) . . . 7

Documentary and cartographic evidence 7

Archaeological evidence 9

Period 2: discussion 15

2.3   Developing the waterfront, c 1700–67 (period 3) . 16

Documentary and cartographic evidence 16

Archaeological evidence 16

Period 3: discussion 18

2.4   Woolcombe shipyard, c 1767–1810 (period 4) . . 19

Documentary and cartographic evidence 19

Archaeological evidence 20

Period 4: discussion 24

2.5   19th-century ship-breakers' yard, c 1810–73
(period 5) 24

Documentary and cartographic evidence 24

Archaeological evidence 26

Period 5: discussion 30

2.6   Commercial wharves, 1873–1998 (period 6) . . 30

Documentary and cartographic evidence 30

Archaeological evidence 31

Period 6: discussion 31

The woodworking evidence   **3**

3.1   Post-medieval shipyards in a wider context 32

3.2   Discussion of the carpentry, shipwrightry and

other maritime-related woodworking evidence . . 34

Aspects of the carpentry employed in the building

of Waterfront 1 34

The reused ship's pump elements 38

Reconstructing 18th- and 19th-century cranes . . 41

The trestle foundation of Building 6 41

The construction of late 18th- to early 19th-century

ship's anchors 46

Conclusions   **4**   4.1   Development of the site 47

4.2   Woodworking evidence 48

4.3   Post-medieval river levels 48

French and German summaries 49

Glossary of woodworking and nautical terms 51

Bibliography 54

Index 57

FIGURES

Fig 1   Location of site and other nearby archaeological investigations at 167 Rotherhithe Street, Bellamy's Wharf, and Bull Head Dock 2

Fig 2   Location of the evaluation trenches, main area of excavation and area of the watching brief 2

Fig 3   View of the archaeological excavation at Pacific Wharf, from the south 3

Fig 4   Graphical conventions used in this report 5

Fig 5   Section based on borehole surveys showing a depression in the surface of the Pleistocene river gravels in the vicinity of Pacific Wharf 7

Fig 6   Extract from William Morgan's map of 1682 showing approximate location of site 8

Fig 7   Extract from Captain Collins' map of 1684 (redrawn), showing approximate location of site 9

Fig 8   Plan showing river walls (W1 and W2) and associated features in period 2 10

Fig 9   Section through Waterfronts 1 and 2 in period 2 . 10

Fig 10   Three periods of waterfront construction 11

Fig 11   Biscuit ware porringer handle 12

Fig 12   Biscuit ware 'cracknell' fluted dish mould 12

Fig 13   Detail from 'Deptford Naval Dockyard, HMS Buckingham on the stocks in 1752' by John Clevely the Elder 13

Fig 14   Frechen stoneware drinking jug decorated with a medallion 14

Fig 15   Extract from John Rocque's map of 1747 showing the approximate location of the Pacific Wharf site . . 16

Fig 16   Plan of timber river wall (W3) and associated features in period 3 17

Fig 17   Land-tie assemblies: keel timber [286], reused as a land-tie beam for Waterfront 1; part of a complex, interlocking, land-tie assembly for Waterfront 3; one of the land-tie beams for the wet dock (S6); piles and cladding associated with the rebuilding of Waterfront 1 18

Fig 18   A tin-glazed ware drug jar 18

Fig 19   Extract from Richard Horwood's map of 1792–9, showing approximate location of site 19

Fig 20   Plan of the timber river wall (W4), the wet dock (S6) and associated features, in period 4 20

Fig 21   Porcelain blanche white mug 21

Fig 22   Land (OA4) to the south of the wet dock (S6): drain (S8); the earlier groyne (S1) behind earlier drain (S2), incorporating reused elements from a ship's pump . . 22

Fig 23   Elevation of a probable crane base (S11) 23

Fig 24   Carpenter's or shipwright's marks, cut into the side of a ship's timber reused as part of a probable crane base (S12) 23

Fig 25   HMS Temeraire beached in front of the Surrey Canal Wharf in 1838 (William Beatson) 24

Fig 26   Extract from William Faden's 1813 revision of Horwood's map, showing approximate location of site 25

Fig 27   Extract from a valuation survey of 1843 (redrawn), showing the layout of John Beatson's yard 25

Fig 28   HMS Queen stranded on the foreshore in front of William Beech's yard in 1871 26

Fig 29   Plan of John Beatson's house (B4), warehouse (B5), building (B6), wet dock (S6) and associated features in period 5 27

Fig 30   Part of the trestle-built foundation of Building 6 and a reused ship's transom beam, part of Structure 16 28

Fig 31   Plan of John Beatson's house (B4), warehouse (B5), wet dock (S6) crane base (S15), structure (S16) and drain (S17) after the demolition of the dockside warehouse (B6) in period 5 29

Fig 32   Construction details of a crane base (S15) and an 'Admiralty long-shank' anchor 30

Fig 33   Detail of the gutter or drain (S17) built of reused elements from a ship's pump 31

Fig 34   A Thames-side shipyard in 1843 33

Fig 35   Map showing the locations of archaeological sites in the London region that have produced post-medieval ship remains 33

Fig 36   The iron strap and lap joint methods employed for joining land-tie beams to posts in Waterfront 1 35

Fig 37   The 17th-century ships' keel timbers, [286] and [273], found in Waterfront 1 and a late 18th-century false keel found in Building 6 36

Fig 38   Two types of ship's pumps c 1780: a – elm log pump, for deck washing and fire fighting; b – chain bilge pump 38

Fig 39   An oak section from a ship's pump reused as part of a drain (S2) 40

Fig 40   Part of a tropical-hardwood ship's pump reused in a gutter/drain (S17) 41

Fig 41   Reconstruction drawing of an 18th-century wheel crane, similar to Structure 15, period 5 42

Fig 42   One of the trestles forming the foundation of Building 6 43

Fig 43   Two trestle assemblies from the foundation of Building 6 showing details of construction and the use of second-hand ship's timbers 44

Fig 44   The art of treenail making in a Thames shipyard . . . 45

FOREWORD

Brian and Steve Fitzpatrick
Fitzpatrick Construction Ltd

As a young company, which started out in construction in 1987 and first became involved with property development in 1995, Fitzpatrick Construction is proud of its record of growth and equally proud to have supported the archaeological work at 165 Rotherhithe Street. This support included an active involvement in helping the archaeologists to achieve their goals on site. It has been a privilege to share in the excitement of the important finds from the dig and our enthusiasm for the work reflects our passion for the sites we get involved in, as well as a desire to build on a reputation for responsible development.

The new building at Pacific Wharf includes 72 apartments as well as retail and commercial space, and has great views across the river. Looking out from here today, it is fascinating to think of the history of the site, with its 17th- to 19th-century timber yards, commercial wharfs, shipbuilders and ship breakers. The activity on the Thames must have been spectacular at times and it is hard to imagine the huge fighting ships that were once moored here, like the famous *Temeraire*. All trace of that era had gone before the South Bank renaissance encouraged a renewed burst of development east of Tower Bridge, transforming disused industrial sites into new residential areas.

We are based in Rotherhithe, where we work from a modern, paperless office to design and build in-house, using our own architects, planning and sales teams. The early occupants of 165 Rotherhithe Street – the Warrens, Shorters, Woolcombes and Beatsons – were entrepreneurs and risk takers. They invested in riverside development and came up with innovative ways of doing things. It is our hope that we may do the same and contribute to the regeneration of the waterfront at Rotherhithe.

SUMMARY

This volume presents the evidence from an archaeological investigation at Pacific Wharf, 165 Rotherhithe Street, London SE16, on the south bank of the River Thames. Combined with a historical study, this has revealed in considerable detail the post-medieval development of a part of the Rotherhithe waterfront, and produced a wealth of data relating to the maritime industries that operated there.

The underlying geology of the site was Woolwich and Reading Beds, overlain by drift deposits of Pleistocene river floodplain gravels. Variations in the height of the Pleistocene deposits, on this and adjoining sites, indicate that Pacific Wharf lies at the south-western end of a large, natural depression, possibly a relict tributary of the River Thames. Thick alluvial deposits that overlay the Pleistocene floodplain gravels had accumulated within the natural depression, when the area was within the inter-tidal zone of the Thames and was subjected to flooding.

In the mid 17th century a timber river wall was constructed, allowing permanent occupation for the first time on what had previously been low-lying, marginal land. Cartographic evidence suggests that at that time the site formed part of Sir William Warren's extensive timber yard, and that in the 1680s it was occupied by a member of the Shorter family of timber merchants. The form of the river wall (which was designed to allow vessels of moderate draught to moor alongside the site) tends to confirm that the site was developed as a commercial wharf, probably in relation to the timber trade. Fairly soon after the first river wall was constructed, major repairs were carried out, probably in response to the partial collapse of the structure. Before the end of the 17th century, silting against the first waterfront reduced its viability and another river wall was built, about 1.0m in front of the original structure.

In the early 18th century, the site was extended further by the construction of another substantial timber river wall, about 5.0m in front of the second waterfront. This would have improved access from the river by creating a greater depth of water adjacent to the site. The archaeological and cartographic/documentary evidence for the use of the site at that time is inconclusive, but it is likely that it continued in use as a commercial wharf.

In the second half of the 18th century, the Woolcombe family of shipbuilders occupied the site and undertook a major redevelopment. The river frontage was advanced by up to 40m by the construction of a new river wall, and a wet dock was constructed behind this new waterfront. Ground level across the site was raised and the overall effect would have been to create a riverside yard that was secure from flooding and a wharf against which vessels of much greater draught could moor.

In the early 19th century, the Beatson family acquired the site and adapted it for use as a ship-breakers' yard. They constructed a fashionable dwelling house overlooking the wet dock and an adjoining warehouse extending down to the river. A large timber building was constructed to the south of the wet dock, on unusual trestle foundations of a type that had not been recorded archaeologically prior to this investigation. This building might have served as a storage facility or a workshop. In 1859 another ship-breaking firm, owned by William Philip Beech, occupied the site.

From 1873 until almost the present day the site was occupied by a succession of wharfingers. During that time, the waterfront was replaced by a concrete river wall and the wet dock was also rebuilt in concrete. The house and warehouse built by the Beatson family were demolished and replaced by larger commercial premises.

The archaeological evidence for the succession of river walls and associated timber structures, such as buildings, drains and cranes bases, has provided important insights into post-medieval woodworking techniques. Many of those structures incorporated reused elements from ships, such as frame timbers, keels, pumps and an anchor stock, which illustrate key aspects of shipbuilding technology.

The artefactual evidence was derived mainly from dumps associated with the construction of the 17th- and 18th-century waterfronts. It includes large quantities of delft wasters and kiln furniture, some of which came from the Rotherhithe pot-house at nearby Platform Wharf. Environmental evidence from the site consists of samples of waterproofing material used in ship construction, including one (hemp) that has not been recorded previously in a British archaeological context.

ACKNOWLEDGEMENTS

MoLAS would like to thank Fitzpatrick Construction Ltd for commissioning and generously funding the archaeological investigation. Particular thanks are due to Brian Fitzpatrick for his assistance throughout the project. The author would like to thank Steve Lock of Lock Brothers Ltd for his cooperation and help during the course of the fieldwork.

Thanks are also due to Kim Stabler, temporary Archaeology Officer for the London Borough of Southwark, for her contribution towards the successful completion of the site investigation.

The fieldwork was supervised by Kieron Heard, and conducted by Julian Ayre, Ryzsard Bartkowiak, Tony Mackinder, Jim Marsh and Tristan Wood-Davis. The on-site surveying was carried out by Duncan Lees, Kate Pollard, David Mackie, Anthony Sibthorpe and Jessica Cowley. Damian Goodburn provided on-site advice and assistance in the interpretation, recording and sampling of the timber structures. Thanks are due to Jane Corcoran for recording the borehole samples and providing advice on the geoarchaeology aspects of the site; Sarah Jones and Joseph Severn, for digitising the site plans and creating the period drawings; Alison Nailer, for assessing the accessioned finds; Susan Pringle, for assessing the building material; Lisa Gray, for assessing the botanical remains and Alan Pipe, for assessing the invertebrates. Thanks are also due to Penelope Walton Rogers for identifying the caulking fibres.

The post-excavation work was programmed by Gordon Malcolm and managed by Peter Rowsome, who also provided comments on text and summaries. The summary was translated into French by Dominique de Moulins and into German by Friederike Hammer. The index was compiled by Susan Vaughan. Fig 38 is reproduced from *The construction and fitting of the sailing man of war 1650–1850* (Goodwin 1987), published by Conway Maritime.

Stephen Humphrey of Southwark Local Studies Library, Hazel Forsyth (Museum of London) and Stuart Rankin provided advice on the historical background. The author wishes to acknowledge the great extent to which he has drawn on the published works of Stuart Rankin in compiling the history of the Pacific Wharf site. Richard Hewitt carried out further documentary research.

1

Introduction

1.1 Location and circumstances of fieldwork

Archaeological investigations were carried out by the Museum of London Archaeology Service (MoLAS) in May and June 2000 at Pacific Wharf, 165 Rotherhithe Street, London SE16, in the London Borough of Southwark (Fig 1; National Grid Reference 535640 180260). The site is located on the south bank of the River Thames, within the Archaeological Priority Zone of Borough/Bermondsey/Riverside, as defined in the London Borough of Southwark Unitary Development Plan (Southwark Council 1995). Fitzpatrick Construction Ltd commissioned the archaeological fieldwork as a condition of planning consent. The proposed redevelopment of the site involved the construction of three blocks of flats and a two-tier car-park.

Prior to the archaeological work on the site, a geotechnical survey revealed the concrete wall of an infilled wet dock, the remains of brick buildings and timber structures, deposits of clay alluvium, river gravels and deposits interpreted as part of the underlying Woolwich and Reading Beds (Geotechnical Developments (UK) Ltd 1998). Subsequently a desk-based archaeological assessment was undertaken (Cowan 1998) which highlighted the need for an archaeological evaluation of the site, and a strategy for investigating the site by means of five evaluation trenches was devised (Fig 2; Seeley 2000).

Trenches 1 and 2 were dug in the northern half of the site by a mechanical excavator. The trenches measured c 3.5m x 2.0m and were excavated to depths of 6.0m and 5.5m respectively. They revealed horizontal dumped deposits of post-medieval date to depths of between 2.6m and 3.2m below ground level. Below these was an alluvial clay/silt, apparently devoid of inclusions. Both trenches contained parts of timber structures, principally vertical piles.

Trenches 4 and 5 were also dug by a mechanical excavator and had maximum dimensions of 18m x 10m and 14m x 8.0m respectively. In accordance with the project design, mechanical excavation continued until significant deposits or structures were encountered. Both trenches revealed post-medieval deposits and timber structures that were thought to be associated with waterfront or dockside activity. Trench 4 also contained brick foundations.

The excavation of trench 3 (at the south end of the site, not illustrated) was stopped when live electric cables were uncovered. This evaluation trench was abandoned (with the consent of the London Borough of Southwark Archaeology Officer) and no further work was undertaken in that area of the site.

The results from evaluation trenches 4 and 5 were deemed by the London Borough of Southwark Archaeology Officer of sufficient significance for further work to take place, in the form of an archaeological excavation and watching brief. This commenced on 30 May, in accordance with a new project design (Howe and Seeley 2000).

Further mechanical excavation linked trenches 4 and 5, and extended trench 5 to the east, to create a single archaeological

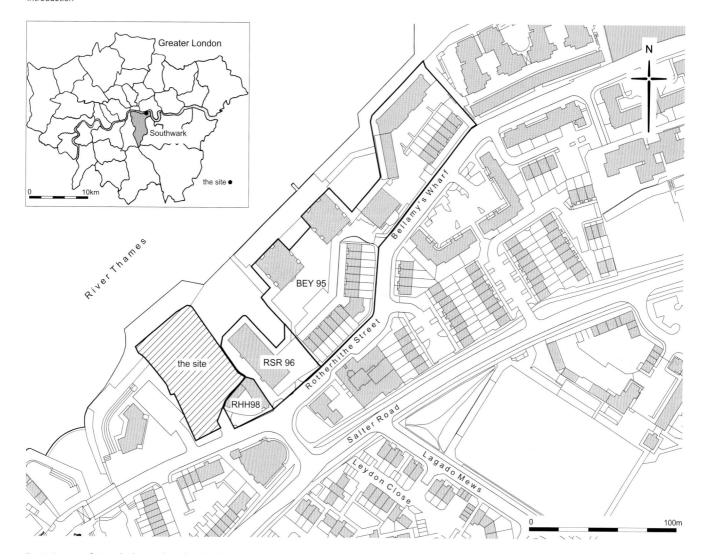

Fig 1 *Location of site and other nearby archaeological investigations at 167 Rotherhithe Street (RHH98; Mackinder 1998), Bellamy's Wharf (BEY95; Saxby and Goodburn 1998), and Bull Head Dock (RSR96; Bates 1996) (scale 1:2500)*

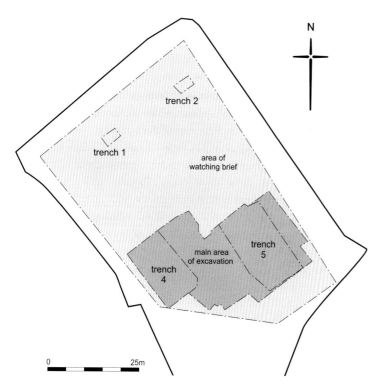

Fig 2 *Location of the evaluation trenches, main area of excavation and area of the watching brief (scale 1:1000)*

trench of irregular plan covering most of the southern half of the site (Fig 2; Fig 3). In this area there was localised excavation by hand and the recording of features and deposits in plan and section. Subsequently an archaeological watching brief was carried out during ground reduction in those parts of the site that were not investigated during the main excavation. Following the ground reduction (to c 2.0m OD, which was the intended formation level for the new buildings) the proposed pile locations were probed to depths of up to 4.0m to test for obstructions. In the course of the watching brief, further information was obtained on structures recorded during the main excavation and a number of additional archaeological deposits and features were identified.

Fig 3 *View of the archaeological excavation at Pacific Wharf, from the south*

1.2 Historical background

Origins of the settlement at Rotherhithe

Rotherhithe is, in effect, a peninsula enclosed by a great loop in the River Thames. To the east is that stretch of the river known as Limehouse Reach and to the north is the Lower Pool. Although there is some archaeological evidence for dispersed occupation and activity in the area during the prehistoric and Roman periods, generally this part of Southwark was too low-lying and marshy to encourage early habitation.

The origins of the settlement at Rotherhithe are uncertain. It has been suggested that the name is derived from the Anglo-Saxon 'Rederheia', meaning a place where cattle are landed (Gover et al 1934, 29). Rotherhithe is not mentioned in Domesday Book of 1066, probably because it then formed part of the manor of Bermondsey.

It is likely that Rotherhithe became a separate manor in 1089 when William Rufus granted the manor of Bermondsey to the new priory (later abbey) of St Saviour, Bermondsey. The first reliable reference to Rotherhithe ('Retherhith') dates to 1127, in the Annals of Bermondsey (Dugdale 1825, 96), when Henry I granted about one half of the manor to Bermondsey Abbey.

There has been a parish church of St Mary on the same site since at least the 12th century, and the medieval settlement at Rotherhithe would have been located near the church. The ground there was slightly higher and dryer than elsewhere in the parish.

Medieval land reclamation

To improve their holdings, the monks of Bermondsey undertook land reclamation in the low-lying areas of their manors, and there are many references in the Annals of Bermondsey to embanking the Thames and repairing the river defences, which seem to have been breached every four or five years. A major breach was recorded in 1294.

A recent archaeological excavation in St Mary Church Street (site code RHE01), near the parish church, revealed the natural ground surface at c +0.90m OD (Jamieson 2002). Given the level of the Thames in the 12th century (c +2.00m OD, Goodburn in prep) this implies a river wall was in existence by the time the 12th-century parish church was founded.

A river wall in Rotherhithe is documented from the late 13th century, when Gregory de Rokesle acquired some land there, called 'Slede', that included a river wall (Douglas-Irvine 1912, 84). The medieval river wall took the form of an earthen bank, running along the line of the modern roads Bermondsey Wall East and Rotherhithe Street. Recent excavations at Bermondsey Wall East (BCB01) investigated parts of this earthen bank, which was partly reinforced by timber.

Despite these efforts, flooding continued to occur throughout the medieval period, even on the higher ground near the parish church. The recent excavation in St Mary Church Street (RHE01) revealed an alluvial flood deposit with a surface at c 1.50m OD, dated by pottery to the late 15th or 16th century (Jamieson 2002, 11).

Origins of shipbuilding in Rotherhithe

Since the medieval period, the history of Rotherhithe has been linked inextricably with shipbuilding and its associated trades and with maritime commerce. In 1355, Edward III sailed from Rotherhithe, with an army of 3500 men in 40 large ships, to fight the French. The ships were merchant vessels taken into the King's service, and some were fitted out at Rotherhithe (Rankin 1997, 2). In 1525 one of the King's ships, the *Henry of Hampton*, was moored there (Blatherwick 1999, 17).

By the end of the 16th century, the settlement had expanded from its original site around St Mary's church along much of the riverside zone, although the inland part of the parish remained largely rural. For centuries Rotherhithe (or Redriff as it was often known) had been home to a well-established community of shipwrights and artisans. These men were, however, excluded from the rights and privileges (including the freedom of the City of London) enjoyed by members of the Guild of Free Shipwrights, based at Radcliff on the other side of the Thames. In 1612 this injustice was redressed when, after years of petitioning, a royal charter was granted to 'the master, wardens and comynaltie (community) of the arte or misterie of shipwrightes of Redrith in the countie of Surrey'. Under this charter, the men of Rotherhithe were entitled to build 'ships, carvels, hoys, pinnaces, ketches, lighters, boats, barges and wherries' (Douglas-Irvine 1912, 84–5).

As a measure of the influence and status of the new guild, its officers reserved the power to survey shipbuilding outside the parish of Redriff. Inevitably this was opposed by the older guild across the river and years of legal wrangling ensued, culminating in the withdrawal of the Rotherhithe shipwrights' charter in 1684 (Douglas-Irvine 1912).

Expansion of maritime industries in the 17th and 18th centuries

During the 17th century, much of London's shipbuilding and maritime trade was carried out in Rotherhithe. As well as the shipbuilders there were mast makers, caulkers, rope makers, coopers and anchor-smiths, to name but a few of the artisans who supplied materials for ship construction. Traders in timber were also prominent in the community, as were the merchants whose goods were transported from Rotherhithe. The parish also supplied men to sail the ships, notably Christopher Jones, the master of the *Mayflower* that in 1620 took the Pilgrim Fathers to America.

In the Commonwealth period (1649–60) the English navy was rapidly expanded, principally as a result of the First Dutch War of 1652–4, and the shipwrights of Rotherhithe must have been particularly active at that time. The first warship known for certain to have been built at Rotherhithe was the 48-gun *Taunton*, launched by the timber merchant and shipbuilder William Castle in 1654. After the Restoration, Castle built two royal yachts at Rotherhithe – *Monmouth* (1666) and *Kitchen* (1670).

The 18th century was the golden age of shipbuilding in Rotherhithe, when its yards were supplying many of the ships used by the Royal Navy and the East India Company. The shipwrights of Rotherhithe therefore played a key role in the development of Britain's maritime and colonial supremacy. The names and specifications of many of the ships commissioned by the Admiralty are preserved in official records but less is known of the output of merchant vessels, which must have been even greater.

Decline of shipbuilding in the 19th century

In the early 19th century the shipwrights of Rotherhithe were among the first to apply the new technology of steam power to ship construction. The first practical steamship, the *Regent*, was built there in 1816 (Rankin 1997, 20) and the first steam warship, *Rising Star*, followed in 1820 (Rankin 1997, 21). The first iron-hulled steamship, the *Aaron Manby*, was assembled at Rotherhithe in 1822 (Rankin 1997, 17). However, the same period saw the beginning of a decline in the local shipbuilding industry that culminated in 1870 with the launch of the clipper *Lothair*, the last large ship to be built at Rotherhithe. During this period of decline many shipyards were given over to ship breaking or the repairing of smaller vessels.

There were many reasons for this decline. Principal among them was the restricted depth and width of the river channel upstream of Deptford, which was thought unsuitable for launching even 74-gun ships, the largest warships built by private yards. It has also been suggested that capricious tides in the Lower Pool hampered the manoeuvring of larger vessels (Rankin 2000, 1).

Another factor was that the Rotherhithe yards suffered from lack of space, being confined to the narrow strip of land between Rotherhithe Street and the River Thames. The opening of the Howland Great Wet Dock at the end of the 17th century, and the subsequent development of the Commercial and Surrey docks, effectively prevented the waterfront yards from expanding inland. The new dock system also took over much of the trade in timber and grain that had previously been conducted on waterfront sites.

The timber ships of the 17th and 18th centuries had been relatively small, being limited in size by the natural shapes and sizes of the available timber. During the French Wars of 1793–1815 it became increasingly difficult to obtain suitable timber; shipbuilders had to rely to an ever greater extent on timber salvaged from older vessels that had been broken up and on imports from distant sources such as North America, Africa and Asia. Rotherhithe shipwrights of the 19th century did not embrace fully the new techniques of iron shipbuilding that would have allowed them to construct the larger vessels that were then required.

Shipbuilding on the Thames was relatively expensive due to the higher wages demanded by local workers, and owners of waterfront sites could get a better return on their investments by converting the shipyards to wharves, factories or warehouses. Two protracted strikes by caulkers and shipwrights in the early 19th century seem to have hit the south bank yards more than those on the north bank and, after the Napoleonic War, Royal Navy orders to private shipyards tailed off steeply (Rankin 1997, 17).

Thus for many reasons shipbuilding petered out, and an industry that had sustained and enriched the people of Rotherhithe since at least Tudor times was at an end. Ship breaking and repair yards helped to maintain the traditional local crafts for a while, but by the end of the 19th century, factories, warehouses and commercial wharves dominated the waterfront.

1.3 Organisation of this report

The circumstances of the investigations and background to the site (Chapter 1) precede a chronological narrative divided by archaeological period and land use entities (Chapter 2). An analysis of the woodworking evidence (Chapter 3) is followed by overall conclusions from the investigations (Chapter 4) and a glossary of specialist woodworking and nautical terms used in this report. Apart from the woodworking evidence, specialist data has been integrated into the chronological narrative.

All specialist data were recorded using standard Museum of London Specialist Services (MoLSS) record sheets for each specialist category and the results then entered into an Oracle database. The pottery recovered from the site was mainly residual and derived from reclamation dumps and is not reported on in detail here; full details and quantification can be

found in the Post Roman Pottery Research Archive (Jefferies 2000). The majority of the ten identifiable accessioned finds are apparently domestic and predominantly dated to the 18th century. None of the items is individually unusual or significant.

The site has been archived by the Museum of London under the site code ROZ00. The archive reports for the site can be viewed by prior arrangement at the London Archaeological Archive and Research Centre (LAARC).

1.4 Textual and graphical conventions in this report

The archaeological sequence is expressed in terms of periods and land use; the land use entities include Buildings (B), Open Areas (OA), Structures (S) and Waterfronts (W). The clay tobacco pipe bowls have been classified according to Atkinson and Oswald's Chronology of Bowl Types (1969) or (for some of the 18th-century pipes) Oswald's Simplified General Typology (1975). The prefixes AO and OS are used to indicate which typology has been applied. Context numbers in the text are shown thus: [100]. The graphical conventions used on the period plans are shown in Fig 4.

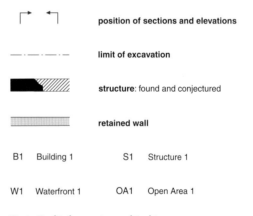

⌐→ ←⌐	position of sections and elevations
—·—·—·—	limit of excavation
▰▨	structure: found and conjectured
▦	retained wall
B1 Building 1	S1 Structure 1
W1 Waterfront 1	OA1 Open Area 1

Fig 4 Graphical conventions used in this report

2

The archaeological sequence

2.1 Geology and topography (period 1)

The natural landscape (OA1)

The Woolwich and Reading Beds, which are part of the Palaeocene series of the Tertiary period, underlie Pacific Wharf (British Geological Survey 1993). A geotechnical borehole near the centre of the site recorded clay deposits with sand, gravel and shell inclusions at a maximum height of -7.66m OD, and it is likely that these clays represent the top of the solid geology.

The earliest natural stratum observed in the course of the archaeological investigation was a drift deposit of greyish brown, inter-bedded gravel and medium–coarse sand. It is interpreted as part of a sequence of Pleistocene river floodplain gravels, deposited at the time of the last glaciation about 15,000 years ago. These gravels were also recorded in a number of boreholes on this and adjoining sites.

The Pleistocene river gravel has a maximum (recorded) height of +0.20m OD, just to the south of the site centre. A nearby borehole indicates that the deposit is about 1.0m thick at this point and is the latest in a sequence of sands, gravels and some clay with a combined thickness of 7.5m. As would be expected, the surface of the gravel slopes down to the north-west, towards the River Thames, with a minimum recorded upper surface at -2.15m OD in a borehole at the north end of the site. However, there is also a significant (and previously unexpected) slope down to the east, with the top of the gravel dropping to -0.85m OD in the south-east corner of the site.

Analysis of data from borehole surveys on this and adjoining archaeological sites (Fig 1) indicates that Pacific Wharf is on the south-west edge of a localised depression in the surface of the Pleistocene river gravels, as shown on Fig 5. Approximately 50m to the north-east of Pacific Wharf, the surface of the gravel drops to a height of -3.05m OD. From here it rises up less steeply to a recorded height of -0.75m OD, just over 200m away at the north-east end of the Bellamy's Wharf site (Saxby and Goodburn 1998; Fig 1, BEY95).

A recently published study (Sidell et al 2002) provides further evidence for this depression. A topographic model of the Mesolithic period river systems in the London area, based on extensive borehole data, indicates that during the Early and Middle Holocene (8000–2500 BC) the main channel of the Thames was to the south of its current position (Sidell et al 2002, 8 fig 5). Pacific Wharf seems to be located on the western edge of a probable north–south channel that might have carried a tributary flowing south into the early river.

Across the southern half of the site, a thick layer of soft, bluish-grey clay/silt seals the river gravel, to a maximum height of +2.85m OD just south of the site centre. The surface of the deposit slopes down to +1.50m OD in the south-east part of the site. Generally the clay is 2.0–3.0m thick. In places it includes bands of a lighter grey colour and towards the base it becomes darker and contains some sand and gravel, suggesting some mixing with the underlying river gravels. The deposit contains plant stem and wood fragments, but no cultural

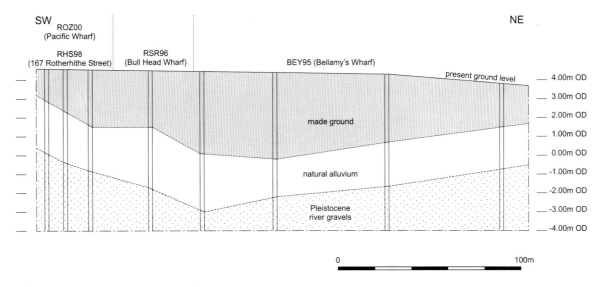

Fig 5 Section based on borehole surveys showing a depression in the surface of the Pleistocene river gravels in the vicinity of Pacific Wharf (for site locations see Fig 1; vertical scale 1:50, horizontal scale 1:2000)

material was seen. Similar deposits have been observed overlying the river gravels on adjacent riverfront sites (Fig 5). They are interpreted as deposits of natural alluvium that accumulated when the area was entirely within the inter-tidal zone of the Thames and was subjected to diurnal flooding by the river.

Period 1: discussion

The analysis of the evidence for the natural topography of the site, together with a reappraisal of the borehole data from nearby investigations, has revealed the presence of a localised depression (perhaps a relict channel) in the surface of the Pleistocene river gravels. It is possible that this reflects the contours of the underlying strata, since deep, drift-filled hollows do occur within the solid geology of the Thames valley. The depression is filled with up to 3.0m of alluvial clay/silt.

The earliest available maps of Rotherhithe reveal that, in the second half of the 17th century, the Pacific Wharf site was at the south-west end of a bay or indentation in the bank of the Thames (Fig 6). This must have formed as a result of the depression in the natural strata. Tidal scouring at this point might even have deepened the hollow, and would account for the apparent mixing at the interface between river gravels and overlying alluvium. Increased deposition at other times within the sheltered bay would account for the great depth of clay/silt alluvium (2.0–3.0m) that accumulated here.

Since the last glaciation, fluctuations in sea level and variations in the rate of flow of the river have had a profound influence on the topography of the Thames valley and the way in which the land was exploited. During the prehistoric period water levels were considerably below what they are today; Bronze Age ground surfaces and evidence for agricultural activity have been found at a height of +0.50m OD in north Southwark, indicating the existence of dry land at that level. In the 1st century AD mean high water spring tidal levels at London Bridge have been estimated at between c +1.25–1.5m OD, but in the late Roman period they declined, to below Ordnance Datum (MoLAS 2000,

93). At some time during the early medieval period water levels started to rise again (as demonstrated by the increasing heights of river defences at a number of sites in the City of London). This accounts for the numerous documentary references to breaches of the medieval river wall (Chapter 1.2).

A recent assessment of the evidence from the City of London suggests that during the early medieval period, mean high water spring tidal level was at c +1.7m OD, with the occasional highest astronomical tides reaching c +1.9m OD, and that by the later medieval period, mean high water spring tidal level had risen to 2.20m OD. Since the medieval period, river levels have continued to rise, so that in the present day the mean high water spring tide level at London Bridge is at +3.9m OD (Watson et al 2001, 27; Goodburn pers comm).

Until recently much of the data relating to river levels in the historic period has come from waterfront sites in the City of London and Southwark, upstream of Tower Bridge. Although river levels in the Lower Pool would not have been exactly the same as further upstream, it is reasonable to assume that with the new evidence for tidal deposition occurring at up to +2.85m OD at Pacific Wharf, the site must have been flooded regularly until relatively recent times. Consequently, this would not have been a favourable location for early settlement or exploitation, until suitable river defences were in place. Even then, it would probably have been susceptible to flooding at times of exceptionally high spring tides.

2.2 A probable timber yard, c 1650–1700 (period 2)

Documentary and cartographic evidence

Cartographic evidence indicates that as late as the 1680s there was relatively little development along this part of the Rotherhithe waterfront. The earliest available source is William Morgan's map of 1682, which shows that the site was located at the south-west end of a wide bay or indentation in the bank of the River Thames (Fig 6). At this point Rotherhithe Street (or 'Shipwright Street', as it was known), which for most of its length ran close to the riverbank, made a sharp detour to the south, before swinging back towards the river further downstream. The road maintained this curious alignment until well into the 20th century when it was straightened, although a vestige of it can still be seen in the modern street plan (Fig 1). Presumably, the road had to skirt around what is assumed to have been a particularly low-lying area of land (Chapter 1.2). Later maps by Pullen in 1720 and Rocque in 1747 (Fig 15) show 'Half Moon Alley' on the south side of Rotherhithe Street, close to the Pacific Wharf site. A public house at the entrance to the alley was known as the 'Half Moon' until at least 1843; the name might have been chosen in recognition of the local topography.

On Morgan's map, the only buildings shown within the area enclosed by the road diversion were at its south-west end, in the vicinity of the Pacific Wharf site. By contrast, the land on the other side of the road (which was presumably slightly higher and drier) was well developed by the time of Morgan's survey, with roadside buildings occupying regular and well-defined plots.

Two years after William Morgan's map was published, Captain Collins produced a map that provides a much better representation of the Thames waterfront (Fig 7). He was a commander in the Royal Navy between 1679 and 1694. In 1681, Charles I appointed him to take command of the yacht *Merlin* and to undertake a survey of the coasts of Britain (Haddock 1989). This took 12 years to complete and during that period he also carried out his survey of the Thames. He was commissioned by the Admiralty to survey 'buildings and encroachments' on both sides of the Thames, from London Bridge eastwards to the lower end of Limehouse, in order to

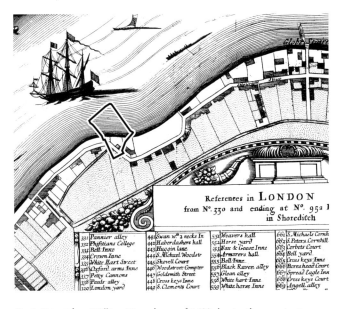

Fig 6 Extract from William Morgan's map of 1682 showing the approximate location of the Pacific Wharf site

identify those that were considered 'prejudicial to navigation and the river'. The resulting map showed the river frontage in unprecedented detail and recorded the names of the occupants of the various riverside docks, wharves and yards. The schedule that accompanied the map recorded the dimensions of each occupied plot of land and stated whether the 'buildings and encroachments' thereon were old or new.

The survey revealed that a 'Mr Shorter' occupied at least part of the Pacific Wharf site, on a piece of land at the north-east end of a much larger holding described as 'the yard in the possession of Sir William Warren'. Warren was the greatest timber merchant of Restoration England, at a time when such men could acquire immense wealth and status. He was a close business and personal acquaintance of the famous diarist Samuel Pepys. In 1663, Pepys (in his capacity as Clerk of the Acts to the Navy Board) made a large contract with Warren for 40,000 deals of Swinsound (Norwegian softwood timber) at £3 17s per hundred, followed by another contract for £3000 worth of large softwood logs suitable for the manufacture of masts. In 1664, Warren supplied Pepys with nearly 1000 mast timbers from Gottenburg and in the following year a contract was made for 3000 loads (or c 4,500 tonnes) of timber. The diarist was a regular visitor to Warren's Rotherhithe timber yard and would have passed the Pacific Wharf site frequently (Latham 1985).

Members of the Shorter family were also prominent in the timber trade. At the head of the family was Sir John Shorter, Lord Mayor of London (1687–8), and (after Warren) one of the principal timber merchants of the time. His son John (born 1660) and his brother Charles were engaged in the same trade, and it is not clear which member of the family was renting part of Warren's Rotherhithe timber yard in the 1680s. There are, however, many references in States Papers and Admiralty records to business ventures undertaken jointly by Warren and Sir John Shorter.

In order to carry out their trade in timber, men like Warren, Sir John and Charles Shorter, Edward Dering and William Wood controlled large fleets, often as joint part-owners of the ships involved (Davis 1962, 96). Although most of their trade was on the Norway and Baltic routes, timber from North America became increasingly important. For example, John Shorter was named in a warrant issued on 11 March 1686/7, by command of James II, to 'naturalise and make free' a ship called the *European* with a burthen of about 400 tons' to carry masts from New England for the use of the Royal Navy. The ship was foreign-built and therefore 'unfree', and at the time of the warrant was in Holland. It could carry masts of 'larger dimensions and greater lengths' than any English-built ship could. The importation of masts from New England began before 1610 and was an important trade from 1652 (when the supply of timber from the Baltic was curtailed by the Dutch wars) until the onset of the American Revolution in the 1770s.

During the Dutch wars the Dutch took or destroyed many of the ships controlled jointly by Warren and Sir John Shorter. For example, in 1672 they seized the *Great Black Cock*, loaded with masts with an estimated value of 28,000 crowns.

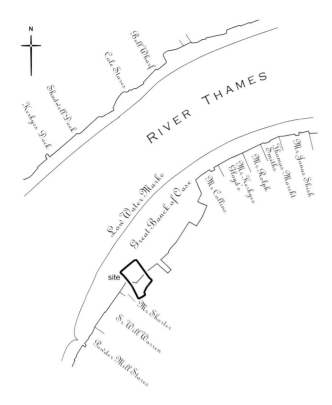

Fig 7 *Extract from Captain Collins' map of 1684 (redrawn) showing the approximate location of the Pacific Wharf site*

A French privateer soon retook the ship. In the following year another ship, the *Black Cock*, was taken, this time loaded with 'masts, oaks, standard knees and other naval goods', as well as tobacco, sugar, oils and logwood. Sir John Shorter and other (un-named) owners had four ships taken and destroyed by the Dutch in the River Elbe, near Hamburg.

Sir John Shorter's will (he died during his tenure as Lord Mayor after a fall from his horse) reveals that among the many properties he owned in the City, Westminster and Southwark was a 'great dock' in his home parish of Christchurch, Southwark. Next to Shorter's house there were timber yards containing warehouses and a crane. These were bequeathed to his wife Isabella on the understanding that his son John could use them 'for and during soe long time as he shall use and exercise in the said yards the trade of a Norway merchant'.

According to the Collins' survey, the curving waterfront was unoccupied for a distance of about 900 feet (274m) downstream of Mr Shorter's yard. At the far end of the bay was Thomas Gould's yard and dry dock, then occupied by Messrs Collins and Graffingham. A rectangular dock was shown to the north-east of Shorter's yard; in time this became known as Bull Head dock. Since at the time of the survey the site of the dock does not seem to have been occupied, it was either out of use or still under construction at that time.

Finally, the map reveals that a 'great Banck of Oase' (ooze), standing up to nine feet (2.74m) above low water mark, covered the foreshore within the bay. Clearly some significance was attached to this feature, presumably because it posed a hazard to shipping. It might explain why the adjacent waterfront was unoccupied at the time of the survey.

Archaeological evidence

Timber river wall (W1)

In the middle of the 17th century, a timber river wall (W1) was built in the southern half of the site (Fig 8; Fig 9). This probably replaced an earlier (perhaps medieval) river wall or embankment to the south, closer to the line of Rotherhithe Street. Since no evidence for the earlier river defence was found within the area of the archaeological site it can be assumed that the riverbank was advanced northwards by at least 30m as a result of the construction of Waterfront 1.

Waterfront 1 was roughly L-shaped in plan, with an overall surviving length of about 25m. Its maximum surviving height was c +2.9m OD, and it is unlikely that the river wall was much higher than that. At the base of the structure was a horizontal, softwood sill beam (woodworking and nautical terms are explained in the Glossary) laid on the natural river gravels at a height of approximately 0.00m OD. This sill beam, which was clearly purpose-made, was rectangular in section (of boxed heart conversion) measuring 300mm x 220mm and (each segment) in excess of 8.0m long. Although the construction cut was not observed it is clear that a considerable amount of alluvial silt must have been excavated in order to lay the sill beams on the underlying gravel, as shown on Fig 9.

The frontage was framed exclusively with oak posts jointed into the sill beam by means of barefaced tenons. The posts were closely spaced at c 600mm centres and survived to c 2.5m in length. Most of the posts were reused ship's timbers, indicated by the presence of relict fastenings. They were of varied conversion type and cross-section (scantling), most being box quartered and some box halved by pit-sawing hewn baulks.

The top of the river wall would have had a series of plate timbers similar to those at the base. Traces of what appeared to be a rot-eroded tenon shoulder were observed on top of one of the posts at c +2.7m OD, possibly giving some indication of the maximum height of the river wall at c 3.0m OD.

The slightly sloping face of the river wall consisted of softwood plank sheathing that was nailed to the riverward side of the posts. Where they were exposed (at the south-west end of the structure) they were of new, hand-sawn softwood about 40mm thick. Towards the top of the sheathing, a reused, tapering, ship's oak wale with a semi-circular cross section was fixed to the posts at a height of c +2.40m OD (Fig 10).

The river wall was supported by a series of horizontal or slightly angled oak land-tie beams (Fig 17). These were fairly regularly spaced and were fastened (by two methods involving the use of iron straps or simple nailed lap joints) to the upper part of every fourth or fifth post. The landward ends of the land-tie beams were held by one or more lock-bars, either recessed into the tie beams or set in through-sockets, retained by pairs of oak piles.

One of the land-tie beams was an unworked log. Another was a new oak beam c 400mm wide by 150–170mm thick and c 6.0m long. It had been sawn boxed-heart fashion from a hewn baulk of oak measuring 400mm x 350mm. Most of the

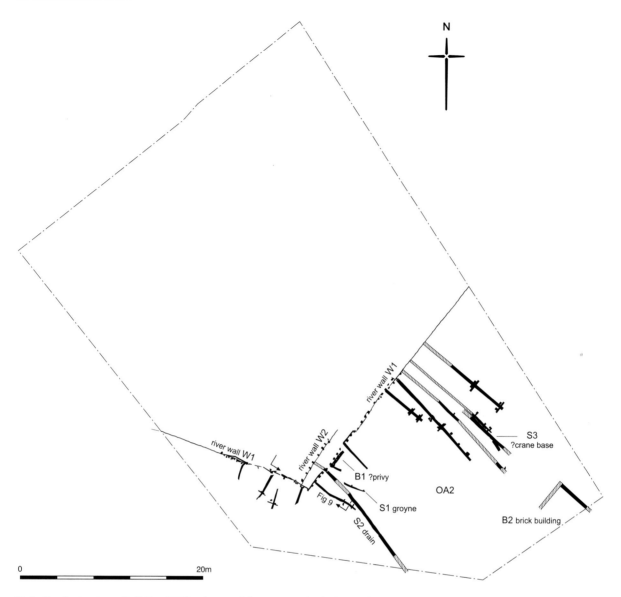

Fig 8 Plan showing river walls (W1 and W2) and associated features in period 2 (scale 1:400)

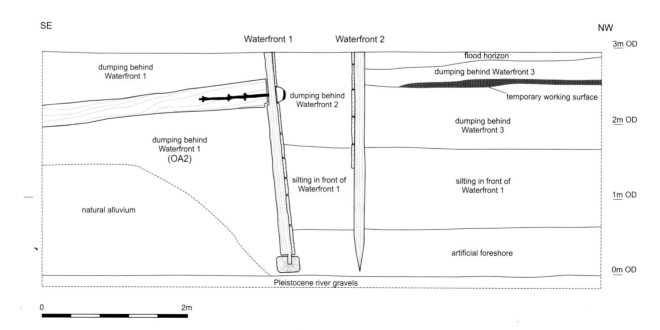

Fig 9 Section through Waterfronts 1 and 2 in period 2 (scale 1:50)

Fig 10 *Three periods of waterfront construction: the cladding of Waterfront 1 is partially exposed, with the domed head of an iron strap used for fastening one of the land-tie beams visible on the wale timber near the top of the waterfront; the truncated remains of the second river wall (W2) can be seen running in front of and parallel to the earlier waterfront (W1); to the left can be seen the end of a ship's pump timber reused as part of a drain (S2), associated with Waterfront 2; the two timber piles to right of centre are supporting the plank revetment on the east side of a channel (S4) associated with Waterfront 3, from the north (0.5m scale)*

land-tie beams were reused ship's timbers, including two keel timbers, possibly from the same ship. One of these [286], measured in excess of 11.60m long and was retained by five lock-bars and pairs of piles. The keel timbers and other aspects of Waterfront 1 are discussed in detail in Chapter 3.2.

Dendrochronology provides some dating evidence for the construction of Waterfront 1, bearing in mind that the timbers were reused. One of the land-tie beams (reused keel timber [273]) had a felling date in the period 1621–57. A pile associated with the other keel timber [286] was felled after 1629 (Tyers 2000).

In front of the river wall, an artificial foreshore was created of gravel and building debris, with a surface at *c* +0.60m OD. This would have helped to prevent undercutting and erosion of the river wall, and provided a level surface on which flat-bottomed vessels moored against the waterfront could have rested at low tide.

Dumping (OA2, phase 1) behind Waterfront 1 and groyne (S1)

While Waterfront 1 was under construction, the land surface behind it was raised by means of a sequence of horizontal dumps (Fig 9). Layers of clay/silt alluvium within this sequence

of deposits indicate that there was some flooding in the area behind the waterfront during its construction. A temporary revetment, consisting of at least two vertical timber piles supporting plank sheathing (S1), was built at a right angle to Waterfront 1 (Fig 8; Fig 22). This structure survived to a height of 0.50m (the depth of two planks) and was at least 2.40m long, having been truncated at both ends. The maximum surviving height of the piles was approximately +2.0m OD. It is interpreted as a simple groyne to stabilise the ground and to restrict the movement of dumped deposits through tidal action.

The soil dumps (OA2) behind Waterfront 1 contained much waste material from the tin-glazed ware (delft) pottery industry, principally biscuit ware. This term is applied to tin-glazed wares after the first firing and before the application of the glaze. The range of vessel forms is similar in composition to those from other assemblages of waste material found in Southwark, notably at the Rotherhithe pot-house which was located at Platform Wharf (PW86) about one kilometre upstream from Pacific Wharf (Tyler, Stephenson and Betts in prep). The forms include bottles, candlesticks, chamber pots, chargers, cups, fluted dishes, small to large jars, mugs, an ointment pot, plates, a porringer, salt cellars and saucers. Of particular interest are a 'snail shell' looped porringer handle (Fig 11) that can be attributed to the Rotherhithe pot-house, and a rare 'cracknell' fluted dish mould (Fig 12). The same deposits also included kiln furniture, in the form of tiles, saggers and trivets. Small amounts of domestic pottery, including Frechen drinking jugs, a metropolitan slipware flared dish and a tin-glazed ware charger were also present. The pottery assemblage has been dated to the period 1630–50.

The clay tobacco pipes from the same deposits are mostly of types AO9 and AO10 dated 1640–60, with a smaller number of type AO8 dated 1610–40. The relatively large size of some of the later bowl types implies that they were probably made in the 1650s. A characteristic of the assemblage is the unusually high percentage of pipes that have cracked and discoloured through over-firing or are of a poor quality, with marred surfaces and imperfect finish. Most of the pipes seem to have been smoked, however, so they were not wasters.

A layer of fairly compacted gravel metalling, up to 0.32m thick, sealed the construction dumps, with a surface at an average height of +3.17m OD. Although it was only observed in section at a distance of 15m behind the river wall, it was fairly extensive and is interpreted as a yard surface. The height of the surface accords well with the proposed original height of c 3.0m OD for the top of Waterfront 1, and it is likely that it sloped down towards the river. A layer of black silty soil up to 0.15m thick accumulated on top of the surface, and is interpreted as a trample horizon.

A possible privy (B1)

There was a small timber building (B1) within Open Area 2, adjacent to Waterfront 1 (Fig 8). A morticed oak sill beam measuring in excess of 2.20m long by up to 320mm wide and 100mm thick was laid on top of two of the land-tie beams at the points where they articulated with the river wall posts. Fragments of planks were wedged between the sill beam and the back of the posts. At least three vertical posts or studs of rectangular section (120mm x 80mm) were jointed into the sill beam. The beam might have supported the wall of an open-sided shed adjacent to the waterfront. Another possibility is that it was the landward side of a small overhanging privy, such as the example shown on an 18th-century painting of Deptford dockyard (Fig 13).

Repairs to Waterfront 1

Fairly soon after Waterfront 1 was completed, some major repairs were undertaken, possibly because the weight of the soil dumps behind the frontage had displaced some of the plank cladding. The western part of the river wall seems to have been rebuilt fairly comprehensively. Some of the land-tie beams of the original structure were cut through close to where they would have articulated with the original posts and a number of new posts or piles were inserted.

At its north end, Waterfront 1 was rebuilt as an entirely new structure of vertical posts or piles and horizontal oak sheathing, just behind the original frontage. At the point where the two river walls overlapped, the softwood cladding of the earliest structure survived to a height of about +2.10m OD. The original land-tie beams (including the large ship's keel timber [286]) were severed so that the new wall could be inserted close behind the original (Fig 17).

The new stretch of river wall could not be observed to its full depth, but it is clear that the raw materials used were almost entirely second-hand, with relict tenons in building-type timbers and oak treenails in both carvel-ship frame elements and sawn-oak hull planking. Generally, the posts used here were less substantial than the originals but it is not known if they were jointed into a sill beam. Since there was no evidence for associated land-tie assemblies the structure must have been self-supporting, which suggests that the posts were actually piles.

Fig 11 Biscuit ware porringer handle [295] (scale 1:1)

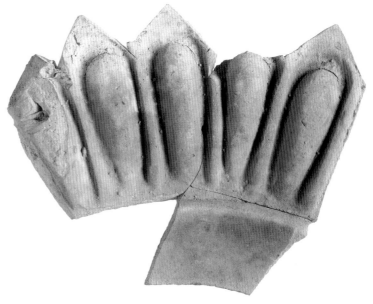

Fig 12 Biscuit ware 'cracknell' fluted dish mould [295] (scale 1:1)

Fig 13 Detail from 'Deptford Naval Dockyard, HMS Buckingham on the stocks in 1752' by John Clevely the Elder (© National Maritime Museum, Greenwich); note the small wooden privy overhanging the waterfront and the clap-boarded wheel crane unloading a timber-laden barge

The construction trench for the rebuilding of the river wall cut through the dumps associated with the earlier structure, and was backfilled with soil containing much domestic refuse including pottery, clay pipes and a large quantity of oyster shells. The pottery was mostly of English origin but included some imports such as a possible Dutch slipware bowl or dish and some Weser slipware. There were also Frechen stoneware drinking jugs decorated with facemasks or, in one example, a medallion featuring the profile of a possible *Landsknecht* soldier (Fig 14). Smaller quantities of waste material (biscuit ware), kiln furniture and post-medieval redware sugar moulds were present. The pottery assemblage is dated to the period 1650–1700.

The clay tobacco pipes from these deposits provide a slightly more precise date for the repairs to Waterfront 1. The pipes are mostly type AO15, dated 1660–80, and are of reasonably good

quality. There are a few examples of type AO9 (1640–60) and AO12 (1640–70).

New river wall (W2)

Over 1.0m of sandy silt alluvium accumulated in front of Waterfront 1, to a height of about 1.7m OD (Fig 9). This is the only possible archaeological evidence for the great bank of ooze shown on the Collins map of 1684 (Fig 7).

Before the end of the 17th century there was a further phase of construction, during which a new river wall (W2) was built about 1.0m in front of the original waterfront (Figs 8–10). This seems to have been a self-supporting structure consisting of vertically driven piles set 0.90m apart, supporting softwood plank cladding. In this case the cladding was on the landward side of the posts.

13

Fig 14 *Frechen stoneware drinking jug decorated with a medallion featuring the profile of a possible Landsknecht soldier [63] (scale 2:1)*

these logs were hewn, and the presence of traces of white paint, tarred hair and lead patches, all suggest that they were originally used in a marine context, probably as elements of a ship's pump (Fig 39). The significance of this find is discussed in Chapter 3.2.

Dumps of building rubble and mortar that sealed the drain were probably laid as new yard surfaces, increasing the ground level within Open Area 2 to an average height of c +3.60m OD. If the interpretation of Building 1 as an overhanging privy is correct, then it would have gone out of use with the construction of Waterfront 2. Either way, it was a relatively insubstantial building and is unlikely to have had a long lifespan.

Brick building (B2)

The brick wall of a cellar at the south end of the site represents part of a building (B2) that was probably constructed in the 17th century; certainly the soft, red bricks that were used are typical of that period. It survived to a height of +4.0m OD and was at least 2.0m deep. Only part of the wall was observed (during the watching brief) and the original extent of the building is unknown, although it is unlikely to have extended much further than shown on Fig 8. The position and orientation of the cellar suggest that it formed part of a building (or range of buildings) that fronted on Rotherhithe Street and are shown on Morgan's map of 1682 (Fig 6). Cartographic evidence suggests that the building survived until at least the middle of the 18th century.

Trestle foundation (S3)

A trestle foundation (S3) in a narrow construction trench (Fig 8) was located in the eastern part of Open Area 2. The surviving evidence consisted of part of an oak sill beam, of boxed heart conversion, estimated to have been at least 6.0m in length. The presence of one redundant 20mm auger hole suggests that the timber may have had some form of limited previous use. At least two vertical posts (both robbed) were jointed into the sill beam (probably at either end), and supported by diagonal braces that were also jointed into raking or 'chase' mortices in the sill. Only one of the braces (a rather waney oak log) survived and was tensioned by means of a small oak wedge in its lower mortice.

The underside of the sill beam was at c +1.45m OD. The construction cut was dug from at least +2.97m OD and by projection it is possible to suggest that the diagonal braces would have articulated with the posts at c +3.20m OD, at about the same level as the original yard surface of Open Area 2. It is likely therefore that nearly all of the trestle foundation was below ground level.

The function of Structure 3 is not entirely clear from the carpentry or other evidence, but it may have served either as part of a foundation for a building with a raised floor (above the level of mean high tide) or as a crane base. It might have functioned with similar trestles located outside the area of excavation, or removed by later activity.

Dendrochronology provides a felling date for the tree used to make the sill beam, of winter 1661–2 (Tyers 2000). The

Waterfront 2 was truncated by subsequent building work to c +2.50m OD, and its original height is unknown. It might have stood to a greater height than its predecessor, in response to increasingly high water levels. However, since it appears to have been less substantial than the river wall it replaced, it is possible that Waterfront 2 was only designed as a temporary structure. Since the full extent of the structure is unknown (due to later truncation) it might also have been a localised extension, such as a jetty, associated with the use of Waterfront 1.

The space between the two river walls was infilled (Fig 9) with silt containing some refuse and building debris, and small amounts of biscuit ware and tin-glazed ware kiln furniture, with an overall date range of 1580–1800. The pressure of these fills would have acted against the sheathing of Waterfront 2.

Yard (OA2, phase 2) associated with Waterfront 2 and timber drain (S2)

A timber drain (S2) that discharged into the river was laid in a narrow trench that cut through the original metalled yard surface of Open Area 2 and breached Waterfront 1 (Fig 8; Fig 10; Fig 22). It is assumed therefore to have been associated with the use of Waterfront 2. The drain was constructed of at least four interlocking and carefully hewn and bored, eight-sided, oak and elm logs, and had a total length in excess of 11.60m. The bore of the pipes was 125mm (five inches). The way that timber was in very fresh condition and retained its bark edge without obvious signs of decay. As oak sapwood usually shows evidence of decay after about two to three years (unless treated in some way, stored in a very dry building or placed in a waterlogged context), it is likely that Structure 3 was constructed within about five years of the felling date of the timber, during the mid 1660s. This suggests that it was in use at the same time as Waterfront 1.

The pottery assemblage from the backfilling of the construction trench includes a range of domestic vessels, principally from the London area, in post-medieval redware and tin-glazed ware, with a suggested date of 1630–1700. There are further examples of biscuit ware and tin-glazed ware kiln furniture, including saggers, tiles and trivets. It is possible that much of this material was derived from the deposits through which the construction trench was dug.

A similar trestle, incorporating an obliquely-cut reused oak sill beam and an elm log brace, adjacent to Structure 3 and at the same level, might have been a replacement or repair to the original structure.

Period 2: discussion

The archaeological evidence for activity on the site in the second half of the 17th century accords well with the cartographic evidence. The obtuse angle formed by Waterfront 1 matches almost exactly with that shown on Captain Collins' survey of the riverfront in 1684 (Fig 7). A brick building (B2), at the south end of the site, also seems to be shown on maps from as early as 1682.

The artefactual evidence associated with the construction of Waterfront 1 provides a fairly close date for the initial development of this stretch of the riverfront. The pottery and clay tobacco pipes from soil dumps behind the waterfront were manufactured during the period 1630–60, and some of the pipes probably date to the 1650s. It seems likely therefore that Waterfront 1 was built during the Commonwealth period (1649–60) or very soon after the Restoration of 1660. There is certainly no datable material that can be assigned with confidence to after 1660.

During the Commonwealth, Britain achieved the largest fleet it had ever known and as a result maritime trade was able to flourish (Wilcox 1966, 16). In these conditions, it may have become economically viable to develop a previously unpromising stretch of waterfront and to reclaim the adjoining marginal land. However, the cartographic evidence, supported by limited stratigraphic evidence for silting in front of Waterfront 1, indicates that the river continued to deposit a considerable amount of alluvium at this point, and it is likely that Waterfront 1 soon became unusable.

In its original form, Waterfront 1 was a strong, relatively expensive, timber-framed structure, built by carpenters using a mix of new-fangled softwood and familiar oak, both new and second-hand. The form of the river wall (notably the absence of front bracing and protruding land-ties) seems to have been chosen to allow small and medium-sized vessels, such a timber-

laden barges or coastal traders to come alongside. The water at this point would have been up to 2.6m deep at high spring tides – easily enough to accommodate such vessels.

Subsequent repairs to the structure (W1) were of a lower standard, using cheaper materials. Repairs were carried out fairly soon after the original construction (perhaps within 10–20 years), but this was perhaps to be expected given the method of construction used (particularly, cladding the riverward side of the posts), and by comparison with other waterfront sites in London where timber river walls typically lasted about 30 years (Milne and Milne 1982; Ayre and Wroe-Brown 2002).

The form of Waterfront 1 is similar to a river wall and a dock found at Bellamy's Wharf, a short distance downstream (Fig 1, BEY95; Saxby and Goodburn 1998). These structures (the earliest found on that site) were built of 200mm square posts, set at distances of about 500mm apart and tenoned into a series of horizontal sill beams. The sheathing of the dock wall consisted of reused oak and softwood ship's planks nailed to the riverward sides of the posts. Large land-tie beams, each of which was a major timber from a ship, supported both the river wall and the dock.

As at the Pacific Wharf site, some of the Bellamy's Wharf land-tie beams were severed, indicating repairs to both the river wall and the side of the dock. Construction dumps were remarkably similar to those excavated at Pacific Wharf, containing large amounts of tin-glazed ware, biscuit ware, kiln furniture, and some distinctive stoneware bottles, with a suggested date range of *c* 1650–70. It is thought that most of the ship's timbers used in the construction and repair of the river and dock walls were acquired during the period 1663–70. The earliest waterfronts at both sites can therefore be seen as broadly contemporary, with Bellamy's Wharf probably being developed slightly later than the Pacific Wharf site.

Documentary and cartographic evidence indicates that the Bellamy's Wharf dock was built by the ship breaker and timber merchant, Sir Thomas Gould. He was a contemporary of Sir John Shorter (whose family probably occupied part of the Pacific Wharf site in the 1680s) and the two men served jointly as Sheriffs of London in 1675. In 1681, Gould and Shorter (both of the Whig party) were nominated for the office of Lord Mayor, but were beaten by the Tory candidate Sir John Moore.

The estimated height of +3.0m OD for the top of Waterfront 1 would appear a little low to be above all spring high tides in the mid 17th century. At Victoria Wharf for example, about 600m downstream on the opposite bank of the Thames, as early as 1585 the height of the river frontage was at *c* +3.0m OD (Tyler 2001). Since mean high water levels appear to have risen continuously during the post-medieval period (Chapter 2.1) we might have expected the river wall at the Pacific Wharf site to have been at a higher level. This implies that the owners of the site did not mind fairly regular episodes of minor flooding next to the river wall, for an hour or two on several days in a month, as can occasionally be found today in such situations.

The construction of Waterfront 2 represented a very slight advance into the river (only about 1.0m of new ground was created as a result) and it is probably appropriate to view it as more of an alteration to the existing waterfront than as a major redevelopment of the river frontage. If Waterfront 2 was conceived as a temporary structure, perhaps in response to some local emergency such as the imminent collapse of Waterfront 1, then it might have been designed with subsequent developments in mind; it was not long before it was replaced by an entirely new waterfront.

The form of Waterfront 1 (which was designed to allow vessels to moor and take the ground alongside) implies that the site operated as a commercial wharf. Most of the area behind the waterfront seems to have been an open yard (OA2), with a metalled surface providing a firm footing in what otherwise might have been very boggy conditions. In addition, there is evidence for a possible crane base (S3). These factors, together with the proximity of the site to Sir William Warren's extensive timber yard and the probable association with the Shorter family of timber merchants, suggest that the site was almost certainly used as a timber yard in the second half of the 17th century.

Indeed, Warren might even have commissioned the building, or at least the repair, of Waterfront 1. He was particularly active in 1665 when he handled very large government contracts for mast timbers. To obtain these timbers, he had to augment his own fleet by hiring 28 ships for the Gottenberg run and 12 for New England (Davis 1962, 96). With business so brisk, he might well have found it necessary to improve the facilities at his Rotherhithe timber yard, and to provide a bigger storage area for those particularly long timbers.

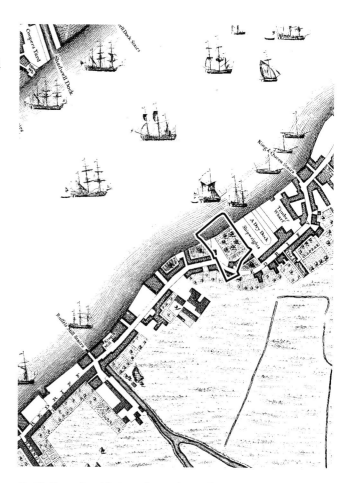

Fig 15 Extract from John Rocque's map of 1747 showing the approximate location of the Pacific Wharf site

2.3 Developing the waterfront, c 1700–67 (period 3)

Documentary and cartographic evidence

The cartographic evidence for activity in the vicinity of the Pacific Wharf site during period 3 is inconclusive. A map of the parish of St Mary, Rotherhithe, by John Pullen (dated 1720, and based on earlier works) shows little apparent alteration to the site since the 1680s. John Rocque's map of 1747 shows a shipwright's yard and dry dock immediately to the east of the site (Fig 15). The dock is in the same position as the narrow inlet shown on the Collins survey of 1684 (Fig 7). A building (or range of buildings) shown at the southern end of the Pacific Wharf site is likely to have been the same one shown on Morgan's map (Fig 6) and identified on site as Building 2. The most significant difference between the maps of 1682 and 1747 is that in the intervening years, the river frontage appears to have been advanced northwards.

Rocque's map represents most of the ground between Building 2 and the waterfront as an orchard or garden; there is certainly nothing to indicate that the site was used for commercial or industrial purposes. This seems unlikely given that the archaeological evidence for period 2 indicates that much of this

ground was made up of dumped deposits of alluvium, crushed coal and hardcore; hardly suitable soil for cultivation. However, if Building 2 was a dwelling house then it could have had private grounds extending down to the river.

Analysis of Rotherhithe parish records of the 18th century by Stuart Rankin has failed to reveal who occupied the Pacific Wharf site before 1767. The earliest available rate assessment book for Rotherhithe, for the year 1754, does not mention the shipwright's yard and dock shown next to the site on Rocque's map. In fact, there do not seem to have been any rateable properties (or at least, occupied properties) in the area of the site at the time of that assessment.

Archaeological evidence

Timber river wall (W3) and associated timber-lined channels (S4 and S5)

At the beginning of the 18th century, there was a major redevelopment of the waterfront when a new river wall was constructed about 5.0m in front of Waterfront 2 (Fig 16). Waterfront 3 was on a slightly different alignment from that of its predecessor, being more parallel with the line of the present day river wall (Fig 1). The method of construction (in the use of softwood sill beams, oak posts and associated land-tie beams) was similar to that of the original waterfront (W1), and it was

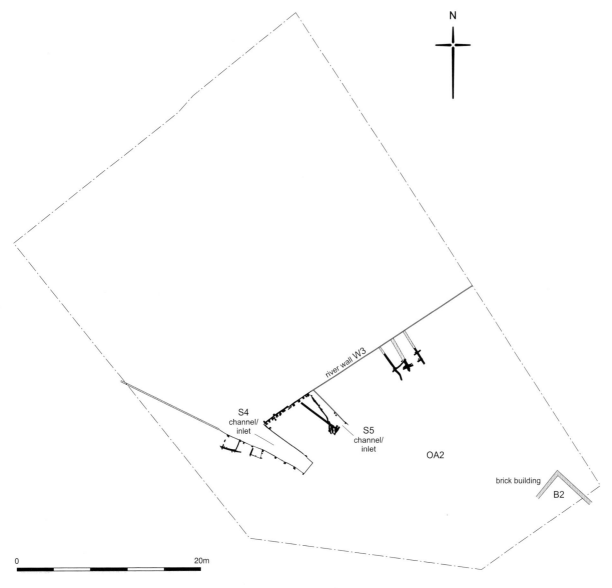

Fig 16 Plan of timber river wall (W3) and associated features in period 3 (scale 1:400)

made almost entirely of reused oak ship timbers, exhibiting relict joints or treenail holes.

Two phases of construction could be seen, although for safety reasons they could not be investigated in detail. Some of the uprights (presumably the originals) were squared, whilst others were crudely cleft. The sheathing was of reused, sawn-oak planking, set on edge and fastened to the riverward side of the squared posts with iron nails. Relict treenail holes showed that the planks were derived from one or more carvel-built ships.

As with Waterfront 1, a reused ship's wale was used to strengthen the upper parts of the river wall. In at least two places, vertical oak posts were notched under the wale and fastened to it with iron spikes. This was probably done to support the wale but also to prevent vessels catching on the projecting wale as they rose and fell with the tide; a similar feature was also used on some ships. The sill beams were at a height of about +0.60m OD and the posts survived to about +2.60m OD, but must have extended much higher originally.

Again, no front bracing was found and it would appear that (like W1), Waterfront 3 was built as an active wharf against which

vessels would have moored, rather than just a river wall. Later in the life of the structure, extra uprights were placed behind the frontage. These were irregular, crudely split, old oak timbers which must have been pile-driven, and were presumably part of a repair or heightening of the upper courses of the frontage.

Although only the western part of the frontage of Waterfront 3 survived, a complicated arrangement of land-tie beams to the east is assumed to have been associated with it (Fig 17). Two of them (a reused building timber and an unworked log) were positioned one above the other with their respective lock-bars being retained by the same three piles. Sandwiched between them was a third, longer lock-bar, that also articulated with another land-tie beam to the west. This one was a twisted branch that was spiked to the top of an earlier land-tie beam (reused keel timber [286]) belonging to Waterfront 1.

The ground between Waterfronts 2 and 3 was infilled with dumps of clay/silt alluvium and silty soil (Fig 9). Within this sequence of deposits was a layer of compacted silt, rich in coal, ash and iron slag, at a height of c +2.50m OD. This was probably a temporary working surface, associated with the

Fig 17 Land-tie assemblies: the archaeologist's left hand is resting on keel timber [286], reused as a land-tie beam for Waterfront 1; the twisted branch spiked to the top of the keel timber, and the group of timbers above the excavator's head, are part of a complex, interlocking, land-tie assembly for Waterfront 3; the large, downward-curving log is one of the land-tie beams for the wet dock (S6); some of the vertical piles and plank cladding associated with the rebuilding of Waterfront 1 can also be seen; view from the south.

Fig 18 A tin-glazed ware drug jar, used for storing Unguentum Populeum [46] (scale 1:1)

construction of Waterfront 3. These deposits contained very small quantities of pottery and clay tobacco pipes dated to the late 17th and early 18th centuries.

Two narrow, timber-lined inlets or channels (S4 and S5) extended back from the new waterfront for a distance of about 6.0m. Unlike the river wall, these structures were lightly built using a mix of oak, elm and softwood planks fastened to reused oak piles. They might therefore have been built as a modification to Waterfront 3. The western channel (S4) extended back as far as Waterfront 2 (Fig 10). The construction of the eastern channel (S5) involved the partial demolition of Waterfront 2, although Waterfront 1 was retained to act as the landward end of the channel. An arrangement of relatively insubstantial land-tie beams and lock-bars helped to support the west side of Structure 4, and probably fastened it to surviving elements of Waterfront 1.

Dumps associated with the construction of Structure 4 contained a large assemblage of domestic pottery with a wide overall date range but a suggested deposition date of 1702–11, based on the presence of Lambeth polychrome wares (type G) occurring as fragments of a punch bowl, teapot lid and a small jar. The assemblage included a piece of a tankard in Staffordshire-type mottled brown-glazed ware with an impressed excise mark with the initials AR for Queen Anne (1702–14). Another notable piece was part of a large tin-glazed ware jug with an applied rectangular strapwork cartouche and the beginning of the Latin inscription U: POPUL. This was the Unguentum Populeum that was used as an emollient for the treatment of burns (Fig 18). Clay

tobacco pipes from these dumps include bowl types AO20, AO21, AO22 and OS10, providing a suggested deposition date of c 1700–10.

Both channels silted up partially, and in places their revetments were undermined and collapsed as a result of the scouring action of the tides. The mouth of the eastern channel (S5) was blocked, and the channel backfilled, when Waterfront 3 was rebuilt. Clay tobacco pipes of type OS11 from an associated dump suggest that this occurred during the period 1730–60.

Land behind Waterfront 3 (OA2)

There is little conclusive evidence for the nature of activity behind the new waterfront (W3) during period 3. Some large cut features of unknown extent and function were observed in various sections, and there was some evidence that the ground surface was raised in places by a succession of dumps or surfaces. There is, however, no dating evidence associated with these activities. There were certainly no structures that could be assigned to this period, although it is possible that Building 2 remained in use at that time.

Period 3: discussion

The dating evidence for period 3 was derived mainly from the construction dumps associated with one of the timber-lined channels (S4) behind Waterfront 3. These contained large assemblages of domestic pottery and clay tobacco pipes that were probably deposited in the first decade of the 18th century. Subsequent repairs to the river wall (W3) are thought to have taken place in the period 1730–60 on the evidence of the clay tobacco pipes of that date found in the infilling of the eastern channel (S5).

The construction of Waterfront 3 in the early 18th century effectively straightened the river frontage at this point, and to a large extent this infilled the bay that had previously been such a prominent feature of the local topography. The effect of this could have been to reduce the amount of silting that occurred and to make the waterfront more suitable for access from the river. The purpose of the two channels (S4 and S5) is unclear. They were too narrow to be entered by anything but the smallest boats, and might therefore have been for surface drainage.

The construction of the new river wall was obviously a major undertaking. There is no archaeological evidence for any associated change of land use at that time, and the site might have continued in use as a timber yard, or at least as a commercial wharf, despite the contradictory evidence of Rocque's map (Fig 15). Building 2 probably remained in use throughout period 3, but there was no additional construction or development of the ground between it and the river (OA2). In this respect the archaeological evidence fits with the cartographic evidence of Rocque's map.

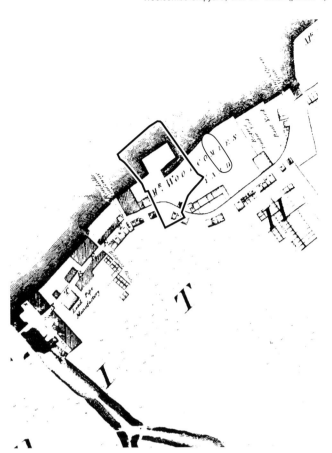

Fig 19 *Extract from Richard Horwood's map of 1792–9, showing the approximate location of the Pacific Wharf site*

2.4 Woolcombe shipyard, *c* 1767–1810 (period 4)

Documentary and cartographic evidence

Rate assessment books indicate that by 1767 the shipwright's yard and dock next to the Pacific Wharf site was in the tenure of the shipbuilder William Woolcombe. It is not known when he first occupied the site, although a trade directory of 1763 does list a shipbuilder called 'Welcombe' at Rotherhithe. In 1767 the dock was known as Bull Head dock, and although the origin of the name is unknown, it might have been a reference to the way in which Rotherhithe Street bent around the site; it does look like the horns of a bull (see Fig 15). The Little Bull's Head tavern stood near the dock from at least 1754.

There is no clear evidence that the Woolcombe family also occupied the Pacific Wharf site in the 1760s. By the 1790s, however, the site certainly formed the western part of Mr Woolcombe's yard, as shown on Richard Horwood's map of 1792–9 (Fig 19).

Horwood's map shows that, by the end of the 18th century, the river frontage within the area of the site had been advanced considerably, and that it then enclosed a wet dock with an entrance to the north-east. There was a range of buildings along the Rotherhithe Street frontage (just outside the archaeological site boundary) but none within the site itself.

The Woolcombe family of shipbuilders occupied the Bull Head shipyard for over 40 years, at one point in partnership with Josh Young. Sun Assurance policies taken out by William Woolcombe in 1781 and 1791 provide details of his property:

Dwelling house	£1000
Household goods	£500
Wearing apparel	£200
China and glass	£100
Warehouse, moulding lofts, summerhouse, saw pits, wheel cranes, sheds and offices in yard	£500
Utensils and stock therein	£400
Utensils and stock in open yard	£500
Dock and dock gates, two launching slips and wharf	£500.

Given the range and probable extent of the buildings and facilities described, it seems likely that the Pacific Wharf site was part of Woolcombe's yard when the first policy was taken out in 1781. The 'dock and dock gates' were obviously the Bull Head dry dock, to the east of the Pacific Wharf site. Although there was no reference to the wet dock that is shown on Horwood's map (Fig 19), this is probably because it did not need to be valued separately as it was, in effect, a continuation of the river wall.

The names of some of the Royal Navy vessels that the Woolcombe family built at Bull Head are known. The largest was *Aquilon*, a 32-gun 6th Rate launched in 1786. Two years later they produced *Deptford*, a 6-gun transport. *Deptford* was conceived as a mercantile brig but was purchased by the Navy Board whilst under construction, for the sum of £1400. She spent part of her working life as the tender stationed at the Tower of London, in 1809. Also in 1788 Hugh and William Woolcombe launched *Sailing Lighter No. 2* for use at Woolwich Dockyard, and in 1792 produced *Mooring Lighter No. 3*, for use at Sheerness. These are the only Navy Board orders that have been traced and nothing is known of the Woolcombe family's output of merchant vessels.

The last family member to build ships at Bull Head, another William Woolcombe, left there in 1805 to become a ship broker, specialising in the sale of vessels for breaking-up.

Archaeological evidence

Timber river wall (W4)

During the second half of the 18th century, the river frontage was advanced by up to 40m, to something like its present location, and a wet dock (S6) was constructed behind the new waterfront, with an entrance to the north-east (Fig 20). Ground level across the site was raised to a maximum height of *c* +4.0m OD by a considerable amount of dumping.

Waterfront 4 was mostly destroyed during the building of the modern concrete river wall and constructional details of its frontage are unknown. Some of its land-tie beams survived (albeit much decayed) as well as parts of two large, reused oak beams to which the land ties were spiked, and associated retaining piles.

Wet dock (S6)

There was also little surviving evidence for the 18th-century wet dock, because it was replaced by a larger, concrete structure in the late 19th century. However, some general indications of its method of construction were obtained during the watching brief. The alluvial deposits that had accumulated in front of Waterfront 3 were dug out, to expose the surface of the underlying gravel foreshore. A dump of chalk rubble, hardcore

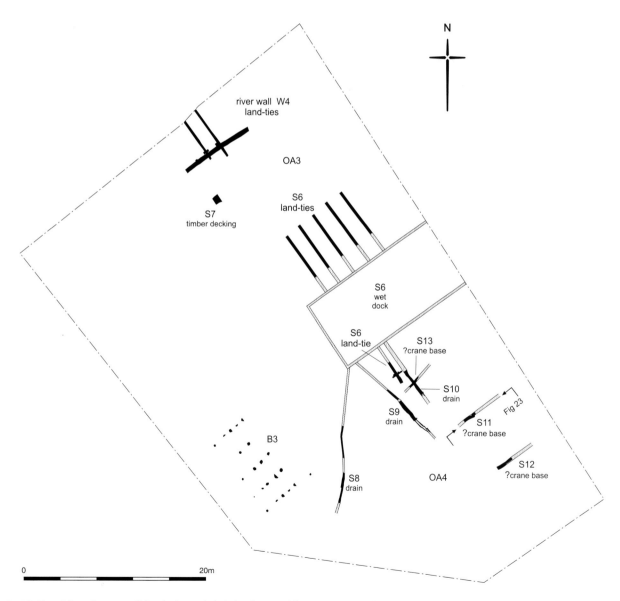

Fig 20 *Plan of the timber river wall (W4), the wet dock (S6) and associated features, in period 4 (scale 1:400)*

and gravel, at least 1.0m thick, was put down to provide a solid base within the area of the proposed dock. At the east end of the dock, the surface of this layer was at c +0.50m OD.

The timber-built wet dock was smaller than its concrete replacement, and probably measured in the region of 16m x 8.0m, with a depth of c 3.5m. It is likely that the wall on the south side of the dock coincided with (and possibly incorporated) the earlier river wall (W3). The only parts of the dock structure to survive were some of the land-tie assemblies (Fig 17). Those that were examined (mostly on the north side of the dock) were minimally trimmed logs, up to 6.0m long and 0.35m in diameter, retained by lock-bars and piles. Some of the logs were fairly twisted and had prominent stumps of side branches. They were spaced at about 1.5–2.0m intervals at an average height of c +2.40m OD.

Dating evidence for this major redevelopment of the site is sparse, and comes mostly from dumped deposits immediately in front of the earlier river wall (W3) and within the western channel (S4). These contained much industrial and domestic refuse. The industrial evidence consists mostly of fine, woody debris from ship breaking or repair. The ceramic evidence consists of a wide range of pottery fabrics and forms, with much residual material but likely to have been discarded during the period 1750–80. The assemblage included a number of noteworthy items. A previously unknown (in London) type of Staffordshire ware with a refined, buff-bodied fabric and decorated with either a metallic black or brown glaze over a red slip has been added to the MoLSS type-series and dated to c 1750–1800. Another curiosity is a near complete *blanche white* mug that, although essentially a copy of a stoneware or earthenware tankard, could be a Chinese-manufactured piece produced specifically for the European market (Fig 21). The clay tobacco pipe assemblage from these dumps also includes some residual material but contains bowls of types OS11 and OS12, suggesting deposition in the period 1730–80.

Fig 21 *Porcelain* blanche white *mug [297] (scale 1:1)*

suggesting that they had originally supported a raft or grid of timber beams that was subsequently removed. This might have provided the foundations for some form of building, which has not survived. A similar method of construction was found at the Bellamy's Wharf site (Fig 1, BEY95), where the timber foundations supported the brick walls of 18th- and 19th-century buildings.

Land (OA3) between the wet dock (S6) and new waterfront (W4), and timber decking (S7)

There is little archaeological evidence for activity on the newly created land (OA3) between the wet dock (S6) and the new waterfront (W4) (Fig 20). The watching brief revealed a small area of truncated timber decking (S7) constructed of reused ship's timbers (Fig 20). Individual beams of 0.20–0.30m width and up to 0.15m thick were held together by 40mm diameter iron rods. The surface of the deck was at c +3.68m OD. It is not known if it was built at the same time as the river wall, or was a later construction.

Timber piles (B3)

To the west of the wet dock, rows of large timber piles (Fig 20), of various cross sections and conversions and up to 1.80m long, were driven into the dumped deposits that sealed the earlier waterfront (W3) and channel (S4). Some of the piles had large iron spikes driven into their tops,

Land to the south of the wet dock (OA4), and timber drains (S8–S10)

To the south of the new wet dock (S6), dumped deposits sealed the dock land-tie beams to a recorded height of +3.80m OD, but no obvious yard surfaces were found, suggesting that the contemporary ground surface had not survived. A sequence of buried timber structures was present, however, indicating intensive dock-side activity in this area.

A drain (S8) was laid in a construction trench at a depth of c +1.70m OD, on an alignment that suggests it discharged into the south-west corner of the wet dock (S6) (Fig 20). The drain was mostly of box construction from softwood planks but, at one point where it had to be passed under one of the land-tie beams for Waterfront 1, it incorporated a bored oak log, reused from an earlier drain (S2) associated with Waterfront 2 (Fig 22).

Two similar timber-box drains (S9 and S10), at a much higher level, also discharged into the wet dock (Fig 20). A small amount of pottery from the construction backfill over one of these is dated 1740–80.

Fig 22 Land (OA4) to the south of the wet dock (S6): in the centre is a drain (S8) that passes beneath an earlier land-tie beam for Waterfront 1; the earlier groyne (S1) is visible behind two sections of an earlier drain (S2), incorporating reused elements from a ship's pump, from the west (1.0m scale)

Probable crane bases (S11–S13)

The trestle foundation constructed in period 2 (S3) was partially demolished during the construction of two new buried trestle foundations (S11 and S12; Fig 20) in the eastern part of Open Area 4. They were oriented south-west–north-east and were therefore parallel with the wet dock (S6). Structure 11 consisted of two massive, debarked oak log braces over 4.0m in length and about 0.32m in diameter, set in a long construction trench. These had tenoned feet, implying some form of morticed sill beam that could not be observed. The brace supported a central post of oak timber left in the round with a diameter similar to that of the braces (Fig 23). By projection it is estimated that the sill beam would have been at c +1.20m OD and the braces would have met the central post at c +4.0m OD, at the assumed level of the contemporary ground surface and above the high spring tide level at this time.

In time, Structure 11 was partially dismantled and repaired by the insertion of another trestle assembly, less deeply buried but in exactly the same position. In fact, the sill beam was notched over the truncated top of the earlier oak log post (Fig 23). This phase of construction was made entirely from second-hand ship's timbers. The central post was probably a reused section of ship deck beam c 0.38m². The sill beam was a reused knight head or bitt; a post to which ropes were tied on the deck of a ship. It had part of a moulding, on what would have been the top end in the ship, showing evidence

for rope wear. There were recesses for iron fittings, relict treenail holes and traces of red paint (on that part of it that would have gone through a deck) all of which demonstrate a ship origin. The presence of red paint suggests that the timber might have been from a man-of-war, since this colour was used traditionally to disguise the blood during action. The braces were formed from the halves of a resawn, oak, ship's frame timber, pierced by 35mm diameter oak treenails. They were tenoned and wedged into the sill beam.

A similar trestle (S12) was located about 6.0m to the southeast on the same alignment as Structure 11. Only one of the braces was observed, and this was a reused oak timber with a rectangular cross section and of boxed heart conversion. The presence of treenail holes suggests a ship origin, probably as a frame timber. The side of the timber bore race-cut marks (Fig 24) that appear to have been cursive letters and numbers, resembling the general style of those found on 18th-century ship's timbers in the wheelwright's shop at Chatham dockyard. The brace was tenoned into an elm sill beam of boxed heart conversion, and tensioned by an oak chock which was itself a reused timber, possibly a carvel-ship plank. Although the whole structure could not be recorded, the construction cut was seen in section to be about 5.0m long, and by projection it is estimated that the braces would have articulated with the central post at c +3.90m OD.

Structure 13 was another massive trestle foundation, similarly aligned and located to the north, close to the wet dock (Fig 20).

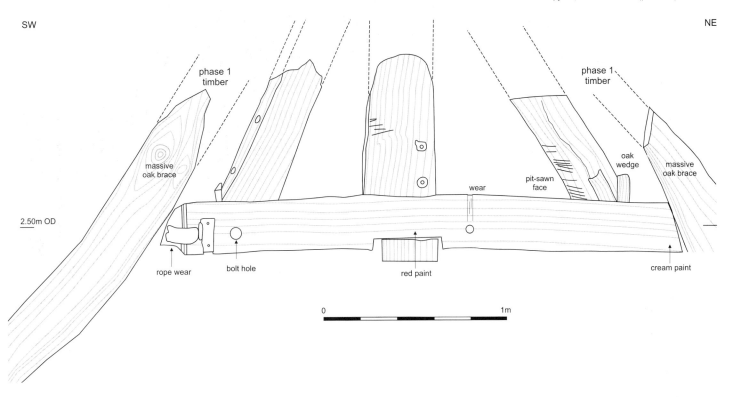

SW

NE

phase 1 timber

phase 1 timber

massive oak brace

oak wedge

massive oak brace

2.50m OD

wear

pit-sawn face

rope wear

bolt hole

red paint

cream paint

0 1m

Fig 23 Elevation of a probable crane base (S11), showing two distinct phases of construction (scale 1:20)

Fig 24 Carpenter's or shipwright's marks, cut into the side of a ship's timber reused as part of a probable crane base (S12) (0.2m scale)

Only one of the oak braces, of rectangular cross section, survived and this too was tenoned into a sill beam that could not be observed.

Structures 11, 12 and 13 are interpreted as the supports for sizeable cranes, suitable for loading and unloading carts and wagons of massive timbers. There is no conclusive dating evidence for their construction. The use of cranes on maritime-related sites and their likely appearance are discussed below (Chapter 3.2).

Period 4: discussion

In the second half of the 18th century there was a major redevelopment of the site, creating the outline that the site retains to the present day. The frontage was extended out into the river, resulting in a larger area of wharfage and allowing for the construction of a wet dock with an entrance to the east. The deeper water in front of the new waterfront would have allowed larger vessels to moor against the river wall. Ground level was raised so that (perhaps for the first time) the site would have been preserved from occasional flooding; at +4.0m OD the new ground surface was higher than the current level of +3.9m OD for mean high spring tide at London Bridge.

The artefactual evidence is insufficient to provide secure dating for the activity that occurred during period 4, although domestic pottery and clay tobacco pipes from landfill deposits suggest that Waterfront 4 was constructed within the period 1750–80. None of the structural timbers can be dated by dendrochronology. However, the documentary and cartographic sources give some indication of the historical context within which these developments occurred.

The map evidence indicates that by the late 18th century the site formed part of the Woolcombe family's Bull Head shipyard. It seems likely that they acquired it, possibly as early as in the 1760s, in order to extend their existing premises, and that they were responsible for the construction of Waterfront 4 and the wet dock (S6). They would have used the Bull Head dry dock, to the east of the site, for building vessels, and the wet dock (S6) for carrying out repairs or repainting.

Horwood's 1792–9 map shows that most of the shipyard buildings (including presumably the Woolcombe family house) were located around the edge of the shipyard and therefore outside the area of the site (Fig 19). This is supported by the archaeological evidence, which reveals large, open areas to north and south of the wet dock. These might have been used for timber storage. A postulated building (B3) supported on rows of piles, to the west of the wet dock, was presumably out of use by the end of the 18th century since it is not shown on Horwood's map.

To the south of the wet dock, a row of three probable crane bases (S11–S13) provide ample testimony that substantial loads, including ship timbers, were being handled on the site. These structures might even be the remains of the wheel cranes described in the Sun Assurance policies of 1781 and 1791.

2.5 19th-century ship-breakers' yard, c 1810–73 (period 5)

Documentary and cartographic evidence

After the departure of the Woolcombe family, the Bull Head yard and dry dock was occupied by the ship-breaking partnership of William Beatson, John Beatson and Brodie Augustus McGhie. The western part of the yard (corresponding to Pacific Wharf) was known then as Bull Head Wharf. After the opening of the Grand Surrey Canal (which had its entrance just to the west of the site, on the area occupied now by the Spice Island public house), it was renamed the Surrey Canal Wharf. By 1820, David Beatson had succeeded to the ship-breaking business, which was then confined to Surrey Canal Wharf; the Bull Head dock was rented to the ship builders Young, Hawks and McGhie. The Beatson family business eventually passed to David's son John.

The Beatson family purchased seven warships directly from the Admiralty for breaking. Their names, original armament and dates of purchase were as follows:

Rotterdam	(50 guns)	1806
Texel	(64 guns)	1818
Tagus	(38 guns)	1822
Treekronen	(74 guns)	1825
Grampus	(50 guns)	1832
Salisbury	(58 guns)	1837
Temeraire	(98 guns)	1838

The ships are well known to naval historians but by far the most famous was the Temeraire, a veteran of the battle of Trafalgar. She played a significant part in the battle and her captain, Sir Eliab Harvey, was named in a vote of thanks in the House of Commons in January 1806, alongside Nelson and Collingwood. The ship was, of course, immortalised by the artist Turner as The Fighting Temeraire, being towed up river to be broken up at Surrey Canal Wharf. An illustration by William Beatson (son of the ship breaker John) shows the hull of the ship at the Surrey Canal Wharf (Fig 25). At the time she was bought by John Beatson (for £5,530), Temeraire was the largest ship ever to have been conducted so far upriver.

Fig 25 HMS Temeraire beached in front of the Surrey Canal Wharf in 1838 (William Beatson) (© National Maritime Museum, Greenwich)

Other Royal Navy vessels purchased by Beatson were *Charybdis* (10 guns) in 1843, and two prison ships. The first was *Captivity*, formerly *Bellerophon* (74 guns), which was bought in 1836. She was the ship that carried Napoleon into exile on St Helena in 1815. The second was *Justitia*, formerly the East Indiaman *Admiral Rainier*, bought in 1855.

There are fewer records of the merchant ships acquired by Beatson, although it has been suggested that he broke up most of the East India Company's old ships, including *Sesostris*, *Thames* and *Warren Hastings*; other merchantmen had previously seen service as naval vessels, like *Rochester*, formerly HMS *Garland*.

A revision of Horwood's map, published by William Faden (Horwood 1813) (Fig 26), shows that since 1799, some buildings fronting on Rotherhithe Street (to the south of the Pacific Wharf site) had been demolished. A number of new buildings had been constructed across the yard, including some in the western half of the site. Although it was then described as Woolcombe's Yard, we know from other sources that the Beatson family had occupied it since at least 1810, when it was described in rate books as 'yard, late Woolcombe's'. It seems likely therefore that much of the building work that took place in the early 19th century was as a consequence of the change of ownership.

A valuation survey of 1843 (Fig 27) recorded the exact layout of John Beatson's yard, wet dock and riverside wharf. It reveals that the buildings extending along the western side of the site were a warehouse (B4) and adjoining dwelling house (B5). A number of other warehouses and a shed occupied the southern part of the site. Beatson also had a larger piece of ground on the other side of Rotherhithe Street for storing timber, which was a typical arrangement among Rotherhithe ship breakers in the 19th century (Humphrey 1997, 28).

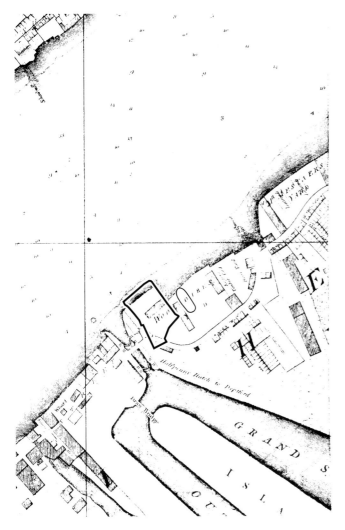

Fig 26 Extract from William Faden's 1813 revision of Horwood's map, showing the approximate location of the Pacific Wharf site

Fig 27 Extract from a valuation survey of 1843 (redrawn), showing the layout of John Beatson's yard

Apart from their ship-breaking business, the Beatson family were involved also in ship repairs and timber imports, particularly of deal boards. In 1839, they supplied 4,062 sleepers to the Taff Vale Railway (Rankin 2000, 7).

John Beatson died in 1858 and in the following year the Surrey Canal Wharf was taken over by William Phillip Beech, a well-established Rotherhithe ship breaker. During his tenure, a number of naval vessels were broken at Surrey Canal Wharf including *Queen* (86 gun), the last large warship to be taken to Rotherhithe for demolition, in 1871. She had been launched as a sailing first rate in 1839, saw service in the Crimean War and was converted to a screw steam warship in 1859. When she was brought alongside the wharf, the ship-breaker's men were caught out by the ebbing tide and the ship was stranded on the foreshore, breaking her back (Fig 28). As a result, Beech is supposed to have lost much of the profit that he had expected to realise, which might explain in part why he closed his yard in 1873.

Archaeological evidence

Regency-style house (B4)

The brick foundations (B4) of John Beatson's house were found to the west of the wet dock (S6), in the position occupied previously by Building 3 (Fig 29). Although heavily truncated, enough survived to indicate that this was a fairly imposing building in typical Regency style, with bow windows at the front and steps leading up to a front porch. The house was of double-pile plan with two rooms at the front, separated by the hallway and stairs, and two rooms at the back. The window bays were supported on regularly spaced softwood piles, indicating that they were probably of more than one storey in height. The foundations seemed to have been built free-standing then buried by dumps of soil and brick rubble, indicating that the ground floor level was above the external ground surface.

Warehouse (B5)

Some brick foundations (B5), abutting and apparently contemporary with those of the house (B4), are interpreted as part of the warehouse shown on the valuation plan of 1843, extending down the west side of the site to the river frontage (Fig 29), and visible on Fig 25, behind the stern of HMS *Temeraire* (discussed below).

Dock-side building (B6)

The three probable crane bases (S11–S13, period 4) were replaced by a large building with a trestle foundation on its west side (B6, Fig 29; Fig 30; Fig 42; Fig 43). Building 6 was over 18m long and (since the eastern side was not located within the area of the archaeological investigation) must have been at least 8.0m wide. Four truncated oak posts (not illustrated) to the east of the trestle foundation might have been some of the internal supports for the building, which probably had a raised floor.

The foundation consisted of a line of at least five trestles set below the contemporary ground surface. They were laid in a long, narrow construction trench at a right angle to the wet dock. Each trestle had a thin sill beam (3.4–3.7m long) into which was joined a central post and flanking diagonal braces.

Fig 28 HMS Queen stranded on the foreshore in front of William Beech's yard in 1871 (from the Illustrated London News)

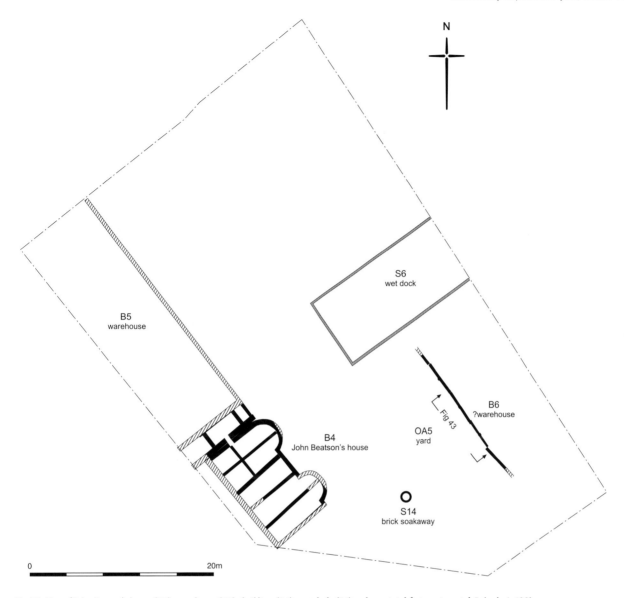

N

Fig 29 *Plan of John Beatson's house (B4), warehouse (B5), building (B6), wet dock (S6) and associated features in period 5 (scale 1:400)*

The chase tenons for the brace heels were cut slack to accommodate wedges driven to tension the braces against the post. The trestles survived to *c* 1.6m high, to a point where some of the braces joined the central posts. Nearly all of the timbers used were of ship origin and probably derived from vessels broken on the site. The constructional details and the marine origin of the timbers used are described in Chapter 3.2.

The only direct dating evidence for Building 6 was a small amount of pottery of 1740–1800 in the construction backfill over the trestle foundation, but this is likely to have been residual material. The stratigraphic, historical and cartographic evidence all suggest that Building 6 was constructed after the Beatson family took over the site in the early 19th century.

Ship-breaking yard (OA5) and brick-lined cesspit or soakaway (S14)

There was no archaeological evidence for the use of the area north of the wet dock (S6) in period 5, but it is assumed to have been mostly open (OA5, Fig 29). The area between Buildings 4 and 6, to the south of the wet dock, was certainly an open yard. Here, a sequence of metalled surfaces interleaved with layers of silt, containing timber debris, fragments of ships' caulking, treenails and iron spikes, provide ample evidence for the ship-breaking activity that is known to have been taking place here in the 19th century. A circular brick-lined cesspit or soakaway (S14) was located in the centre of the yard, perhaps inside a small out-house or privy (Fig 29).

Crane base (S15)

After Building 6 went out of use and was demolished, two dockside structures (S15 and S16) were built within a single large construction trench (Fig 31). Structure 15 is interpreted as the base of a crane. It consisted of two parallel softwood sill beams 4.5m in length, formed from the halves of a composite anchor stock (Fig 32; Chapter 3.2). These were joined by two nailed-on planks of oak and elm and supported an assembly of *c* 200mm square vertical oak posts and diagonal braces.

Fig 30 *View from the south of part of the trestle-built foundation of Building 6 (foreground) and a large, horizontal timber, a reused ship's transom beam (centre), forming part of Structure 16*

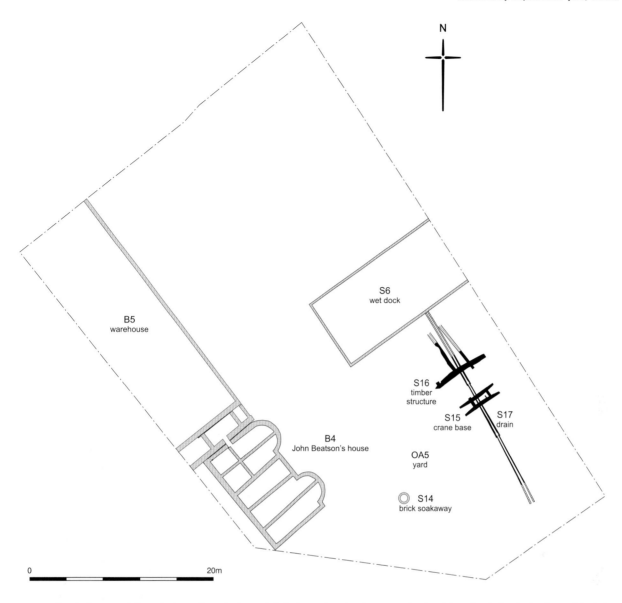

Fig 31 *Plan of John Beatson's house (B4), warehouse (B5), wet dock (S6) crane base (S15), structure (S16) and drain (S17) after the demolition of the dockside warehouse (B6) in period 5 (scale 1:400)*

The northern sill beam was morticed to receive four unpegged, stub-tenoned oak posts. The southern sill beam held two similar posts, each supported by a diagonal oak brace that was spiked to the sill beam. The timbers were probably all reused, or (in the case of the two planks) offcuts. The nature of the carpentry, particularly in the use of unpegged stub-tenons and the simple butting and spiking of the braces to the sill beams, was quite crude and in some respects resembles the trestle foundation of Building 6.

Timber structure (S16)

Structure 16 was built between the crane base (S15) and the wet dock (S6) (Fig 31). Two substantial, reused timber beams overlapped with and were spiked to a large, curving timber that had originally been part of a ship's transom beam (Fig 30). The function of this structure is uncertain;

it might have been part of the foundation raft for a dockside building, or a land-tie assembly associated with a relatively late repair to, or reinforcement of, the south wall of the wet dock. The construction dumps sealing both of these structures (S15 and S16) included much residual material of the 17th and 18th centuries and small amounts of pottery dated 1807–50.

Timber gutter or drain (S17)

After the demolition of Structures 15 and 16, a timber gutter or drain with a plank lid was laid across the east end of the yard (OA5), to discharge into the wet dock (S6) (Fig 31; Fig 33). It was constructed from at least three sections of a ship's pump pipe, of tropical hardwood (Chapter 3.2). It was sealed by another metalled surface, indicating the continued build-up of the ground surface of the ship-breaking yard.

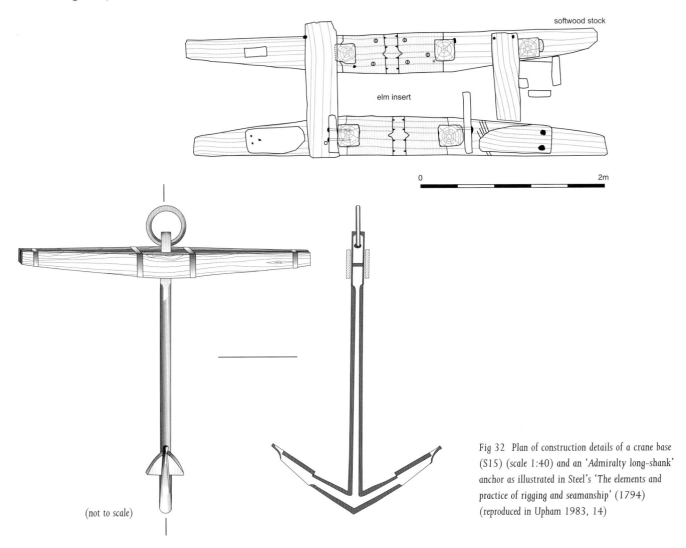

softwood stock

elm insert

0   2m

(not to scale)

Fig 32 Plan of construction details of a crane base
(S15) (scale 1:40) and an 'Admiralty long-shank'
anchor as illustrated in Steel's 'The elements and
practice of rigging and seamanship' (1794)
(reproduced in Upham 1983, 14)

Period 5: discussion

No precise dating evidence was recovered. Once again,
historical sources and analysis of the site stratigraphy have
been used to elucidate the sequence of events that occurred
in period 5.

When the Beatson family acquired the Pacific Wharf site
in the early 19th century they set about adapting it to suit
their own requirements. They had a fashionable house built
in the contemporary style (B4) with windows overlooking
their new yard and dock. Adjoining the house was a sturdy
brick-built warehouse (B5) extending to the river; its
riverward face can be seen on Fig 25, behind the stern of
HMS Temeraire. The building was four storeys high and had
large doors on every level to facilitate the transfer of goods
and material between the warehouse and vessels moored
against the river wall.

At least one large timber building was erected during
the period that the Beatsons occupied the site. The dating
evidence for Building 6 is inconclusive, but since it was not
shown on Faden's 1813 edition of Horwood's map (Fig 26)
it was probably built soon after that date. It is unlikely that
the building would have lasted more than 25 years, which
accounts for it not being shown on the valuation plan of

1843 (Fig 27). The form of the building cannot be deduced
from the available evidence and it might have been little more
than a covered area of raised decking, perhaps for storing
timber or for use as a workshop.

After Building 6 was demolished, a crane (S15) was set
up in the ship-breakers' yard, perhaps the crane bought by
the Beatsons from a Mr Lloyd in 1832, for the sum of £115
(Rankin 2000, 7).

2.6 Commercial wharves, 1873–1998 (period 6)

Documentary and cartographic evidence

The departure of William Beech marked the end of ship breaking
at Surrey Canal Wharf and the site was occupied subsequently by
a succession of wharfingers. The Ordnance Survey map of 1894
reveals that, by the end of the 19th century, the house built by
the Beatson family had been demolished and warehouses and
workshops covered the site. It is likely that by that date the river
wall and the dry dock had been rebuilt in concrete.

Fig 33 *Detail of the gutter or drain (S17) built of reused elements from a ship's pump; the junction of two sections has been repaired with a lead sheet. View from the south (0.5m scale)*

In the early 20th century the site became a slate wharf, receiving shiploads of roofing materials from the Dinorwic quarries in North Wales. As late as 1998 the site was still handling slate, albeit brought to London by road. The wet dock remained in use until at least 1914, but by the 1950s, when the site was known as Surrey Commercial Wharf, the dock had been infilled. It was renamed Pacific Wharf in the late 1990s.

Archaeological evidence

Concrete river wall (W5)

After the demolition of Beatson's house (B4) and adjoining warehouse (B5), a layer of rubble and industrial waste, including much iron slag, was dumped across the whole site, raising ground level by up to 0.80m. This formed the make-up for a concrete slab with a surface at c +4.6m OD. The metalworking waste probably came from the Thames Bank Ironworks that operated in the mid 19th century on the Bull Head Dock site (next to the Pacific Wharf site).

At the same time, the land-tie beams of Waterfront 4 were severed during the construction of a new, concrete river wall (W5, not illustrated). Similarly, the land-tie beams of the timber wet dock (S6) were truncated and its timber walls were dismantled, when the dock was enlarged and rebuilt in concrete.

Period 6: discussion

The demise of shipbuilding, breaking and repair at the Pacific Wharf site, and the subsequent change of use of the site to warehousing and wharfage, are typical of developments on the Rotherhithe waterfront in the mid to late 19th century. The maritime industries relocated downriver or to other parts of Britain, and the former dockyards were adapted to other, often fairly transitory, functions. Today, with much of the south bank of the River Thames redeveloped for housing, there is little visible evidence for former industry. Archaeological investigation in advance of redevelopment can often provide the only means of bringing to light the remains of Rotherhithe's rich maritime heritage.

3

The woodworking evidence

Damian Goodburn

3.1 Post-medieval shipyards in a wider context

The expansion of European maritime trade in the post-medieval period, to cover the whole globe, was a factor of huge importance in the shaping of the modern world, with its linked features of political, economic and cultural conquest. None of this would have been possible without the considerable advances that were made in shipbuilding technology, in which the shipwrights of London played a major role. The historical sources for the development of the shipbuilding industry have been studied for many years (eg Banbury 1971; Lavery 1991), as have the remains of post-medieval shipwrecks and their cargoes. However, the archaeology of the land infra-structure that made all this possible has been much neglected, particularly outside the realms of the royal dockyards, which have received occasional attention (eg Courtney 1973; Courtney 1974). An engraving of a Thames-side shipyard published in 1843 must have been a view typical of many large shipbuilding and repair yards, from the 17th century until the late 19th century (Fig 34; Dodd 1843, 458, fig 20). A few archaeological observations have been made of parts of the industrial shores of east London, by dedicated individuals with few resources, such as the late Brian Gill working in Deptford. Research by local historian Stuart Rankin has been of great value to archaeologists studying the maritime history of Rotherhithe and much of his work has direct relevance to the site at Pacific Wharf (Rankin 2000; Rankin (ed) 2000).

During the late 1980s and early 1990s, archaeological work on a small number of waterfront sites in the City of London and north Southwark provided some information on post-medieval waterfront carpentry and aspects of shipwrightry. Finds of reused boat, barge and ship timbers from those sites have been analysed, and detailed summaries published (Goodburn 1991; Marsden 1996). Records of the post-medieval carpentry found have recently been analysed systematically and will be published shortly (Goodburn in prep).

By the mid 1990s the pace of archaeological work in the maritime industrial zone of Greater London had increased greatly, with several systematic excavations and watching briefs yielding valuable results relevant to the study of the woodwork found in these waterlogged areas (Fig 35). One of the first excavations to be published was carried out by MoLAS at Bellamy's Wharf in 1995, just downstream of Pacific Wharf (Fig 1, BEY95; Saxby and Goodburn 1998). The analysis of the shipwrightry and carpentry found at that site has provided much comparable information for the study of the material from Pacific Wharf, in such areas as the use of particular materials, tools, techniques and fastenings. In 1996, work at Victoria Wharf, Limehouse (VIT96) also yielded comparable evidence, for the change from medieval to post-medieval styles of waterfront carpentry, and some indication of the nature of shipyard infrastructure in the late

Fig 34 *A Thames-side shipyard in 1843; note the pile of curved logs in the foreground (Dodd 1843, 458, fig 20)*

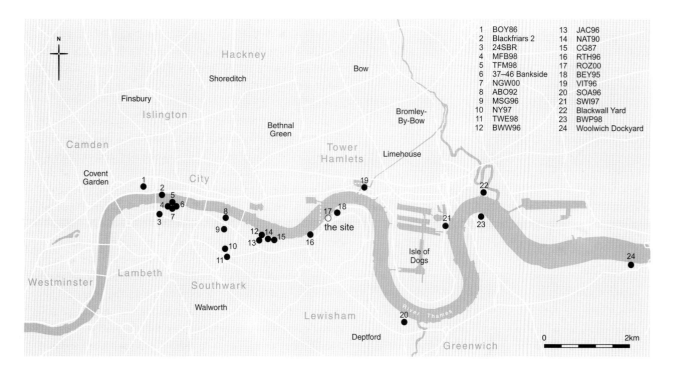

1	BOY86	13	JAC96
2	Blackfriars 2	14	NAT90
3	24SBR	15	CG87
4	MFB98	16	RTH96
5	TFM98	17	ROZ00
6	37–46 Bankside	18	BEY95
7	NGW00	19	VIT96
8	ABO92	20	SOA96
9	MSG96	21	SWI97
10	NY97	22	Blackwall Yard
11	TWE98	23	BWP98
12	BWW96	24	Woolwich Dockyard

Fig 35 *Map showing the locations of archaeological sites in the London region that have produced post-medieval ship remains (scale 1:40,000)*

16th century (Tyler 2001). Other early industrialised maritime woodwork and waterfront carpentry, found at Pier head, Isle of Dogs (SWI97), was broadly contemporary with the later evidence from the Pacific Wharf site (Pitt and Goodburn in prep).

This accumulating body of information from London has allowed some of the key differences in ship, boat and barge building between the medieval and post-medieval periods to be distinguished, although much more work is required (Goodburn 1999; Goodburn 2000). It is already clear that there were considerable differences between the approaches used by both carpenters and shipwrights working on the waterfront in medieval London and those of the 16th to 18th centuries, as the summary presented here will help to show. Surprisingly perhaps, aspects of maritime related woodwork, shipwrightry and foreshore carpentry from the early industrial age up to the mid 19th century are still little known in detail. Analysis of some of the latest woodwork found at Pacific Wharf has illuminated an important specialised craft, that of ship's pump making, to set along side earlier evidence from this site and elsewhere (Oertling 1996).

Survey work on the Thames foreshore has also yielded relevant evidence that is gradually being collated and prepared for publication (G Milne, pers comm). Initial surveys and limited excavations have been carried out too at early industrial and post-medieval maritime sites elsewhere, in the north west of England (Stammers 1999) and at an 18th-century site at Bucklers Hard in Hampshire (Adams in prep). However, these results have yet to be published in detail. In the nearer parts of continental Europe, recent work, as at a number of sites in the Netherlands and at Copenhagen, is also shedding light on the infrastructure of post-medieval shipbuilding and related trades, though much of this work also awaits publication (J Gavronski, pers comm; Lemee 1997).

Finally, the importance of the post-medieval maritime industrial zone as part of the regional archaeological resource has now been recognised formally, and work there seen as a priority, by curatorial bodies responsible for the Thames Estuary region as far upstream as Tower Bridge (English Heritage 1998; Williams and Brown 1999, 21). The convenient boundary of Tower Bridge does not, however, define the limits of the post-medieval maritime industrial zone, as several excavations above Tower Bridge (as at the former City of London Boys School, BOY86) have yielded key evidence (Goodburn 1991, 112). More recent excavations, on the site of the Millennium footbridge in Southwark, have also revealed important evidence in the form of the first recognised remains of a 'western barge' (Goodburn 2002). These vessels were very distinctively built and were used for the carriage of goods, such as timber, between the middle estuary and the freshwater head of navigation of the Thames. They would have been frequent visitors to the river frontage at the Pacific Wharf site, to bring in new raw materials such as timber, and to carry away second-hand materials derived from ship breaking and repair, such as timber, firewood and metals.

3.2 Discussion of the carpentry, shipwrightry and other maritime-related woodworking evidence

Aspects of the carpentry employed in the building of Waterfront 1

Some post-medieval developments in waterfront construction and carpentry

In its original form, Waterfront 1 was prefabricated off-site as a timber-framed structure, with oak posts that were barefaced tenoned into softwood sill beams (woodworking and nautical terms are explained in the Glossary). The structure was built to have a slight batter, sloping at about 5°. This was a new feature of waterfront construction, not typically employed in the medieval timber river or dock walls that have been recorded in London. It became common during the post-medieval period for both timber and brick river and dock walls, and was presumably used to give a little extra stability to the frontage.

No traces of the distinctive crossing saw marks, known from trestle-sawing methods used in constructing medieval structures, were found on any of the exposed timbers associated with Waterfront 1. However, clear marks left by pit-sawing survived on some of the land-tie beams. It has recently become clear that a form of pit-sawing was already in use for some waterfront carpentry in London by at least as early as c 1410 (Goodburn 2002; Goodburn in prep).

A post-medieval development to reduce costs in joining in land-tie assemblies

The land-ties were fitted to every fourth or fifth post using two different methods (Fig 36). In the first method, the joint was made by cutting a shallow shoulder in the post for the riverward end of the tie beam to rest on, and then the connection was made with a wrought iron strap. The second method involved lapping the end of the land-tie around the side of the post and fastening it with two iron spikes. Both these methods have been recorded on other post-medieval waterfront sites in London. At Victoria Wharf, Limehouse, the iron strap method was used as early as 1585 (Goodburn 2001, 73). It was also used for some of the land-tie/post joints at Bellamy's Wharf (Fig 1, BEY95) in the 1660s. At both sites the valuable iron straps were subsequently salvaged, but at Bellamy's Wharf, the shanks of the securing staples survived in the timber to indicate the previous use of the straps.

The iron-strapped connections would have been very strong, whilst the lapped and spiked examples would have been relatively weak. However, both methods would have required little if any prefabrication and had the advantage of flexibility and speed of execution. This would have made them cheaper than the fully framed, truss-like land-tie assemblies used in many medieval river and dock walls. This cost-effective

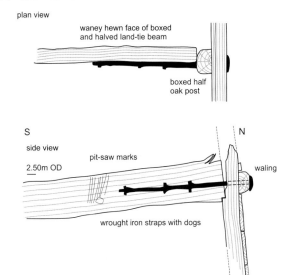

IRON STRAP METHOD

plan view

waney hewn face of boxed
and halved land-tie beam

boxed half
oak post

S   N

side view

pit-saw marks

2.50m OD

waling

wrought iron straps with dogs

0   2m

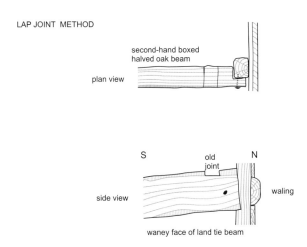

LAP JOINT METHOD

second-hand boxed
halved oak beam

plan view

S   old   N
     joint

side view   waling

waney face of land tie beam

Fig 36 *The iron strap and lap joint methods employed for joining land-tie beams to posts in Waterfront 1 (scale 1:40)*

approach to aspects of timber framing through the use of iron strapping has also been found used in 'land' carpentry, in buildings of broadly contemporary date in the City of London. Examples include the rebuilding in the 1620s of the spire of St Ethelburga's church and the construction in 1683 of king-post roof trusses in the Middle Temple Gatehouse (Goodburn and Minkin 1999; Goodburn and Minkin 2000).

The fact that the cladding of the river wall was nailed to the front or riverward faces of the posts would also have facilitated repair and speed of assembly. It must, however, have produced a weaker structure than the older method, of placing the cladding on the landward side of the posts so that the pressure of the landfill could not push it off. This feature of comparative weakness must be contrasted with the massive strength of some of the land-tie assemblies, including one that was over 11.6m long and had five lock-bars and pairs of anchor stakes.

The cladding of Waterfront 1 and the use of new raw materials as a response to urban timber shortages

In many ways, the method of cladding used on Waterfront 1 also exemplifies changes in London carpentry practice that took place in the post-medieval period. The cladding was mainly of new, hand-sawn softwood, secured to the posts with two or three iron nails. This weaker method of sheathing a water frontage is now well known from several 17th-century and later London waterfront sites, such as at the Giant Knot Garden in Rotherhithe Street (RTH96) and at Greenwich Reach (NWS97) in Deptford (Goodburn 1996; Divers in prep). The practice of applying the sheathing to the riverward face of the posts might reflect the carvel shipbuilding practice so in evidence in the London area at that time. By this method, hull planks were fastened to the faces of the framing timbers, although this was mainly done with oak treenails rather than iron nails. Another echo of shipbuilding practice was the use of the oak waling beam that stood out proud of the main sheathing (see Fig 10; Fig 36). Again, this was not a feature of medieval waterfront carpentry but a post-medieval innovation.

The sill beam of Waterfront 1 was also of softwood, which at that time had to be imported. It was obtained mainly from Norway or the northern Baltic countries, although some New World softwood was also coming to London as early as 1609 (Banbury 1971, 57). Here, that the site was apparently owned by Sir William Warren, a well-known importer of softwood timber from Scandinavia and the Baltic, must be relevant. Indeed, it is probable that the softwood timber used in this structure was pine from Warren's own stock. The lesson given by Warren to Samuel Pepys on 23 June 1662 about the various sorts of softwood 'deals' that were coming to London at that time probably happened close by (Latham 1985).

In medieval and many 16th-century river and dock frontages, the sheathing was of native timbers such as sawn planking of oak or elm, so the use of so much softwood for the construction of Waterfront 1 is noteworthy.

Whilst the concept of an increasing post-medieval shortage of home-grown timber has clearly been over-played over the last 100 years (Rackham 1976, 99), the demands placed on regional timber supplies in the London hinterland were great from the late 16th century onward. Oak and elm were in great demand for expanding local shipbuilding and other purposes. Evidence from the London waterfront zone clearly shows that experiments were being made as early as the mid 16th century, with the use of imported softwood by London carpenters (Goodburn in prep). Even where new oak was still used for sheathing, it was often of poor quality, sappy off-cuts from the outside of sawn logs and baulks, that were sold on by shipyards (Goodburn 2001, 73).

The use of softwood planks for cladding Waterfront 1 may have been a response to local shortages of home-grown timber in the mid 17th century, with issues of price and convenience also playing a part. The softwood would also have been quicker and easier to fit because it could be cut and bored with hand tools more rapidly than oak or elm, the harder native alternatives. Another great advantage of the coniferous timber was that it was more readily available in long lengths and with little taper, and it had a straighter grain; the sill beams for Waterfront 1 were over 8.0m long for example. Timbers of this length and over were available in oak or elm, but would have been particularly expensive unless second-hand, and for frontage sills they were apparently used in shorter, cheaper lengths (Goodburn 2001, 74). This combination of moderate length new oak, reused oak timber and long softwood beams has also been found in some late 17th-century building carpentry in London, such as the roofs of Middle Temple Gatehouse (Goodburn and Minkin 2000). A similar pattern of the use of mixed materials can be seen in the solid timber-framed river wall constructed downstream of the River Fleet in the early 1670s, found at the former City of London Boys School (BOY86; Goodburn 1992). We may see here the beginning of the conversion of London's carpenters to the use of imported softwoods for nearly all carpentry work by the 18th century. On the waterfront, the culmination of this process is exemplified by structures such as the entirely pine dry dock of c 1780–1800, excavated in 1997 at West India Docks (SWI97; Pitt and Goodburn in prep).

Use of Waterfront 1

A distinctive feature of Waterfront 1 is that it was built without any substantial projections into the river, such as front braces, which were often used with river walls that were not used directly by vessels. It therefore seems very likely that the structure functioned as some kind of wharf frontage, where vessels of shallow draft, such as barges, small coastal traders and fishing craft, could come alongside to load or unload materials (Fig 41). The way that the frontage was repaired, with driven piles, suggests that for a number of years it continued to be used in such a way that access was required from the water. It was far more typical, ever since early medieval times, to use raking shores or front braces to repair frontages that were principally acting as river walls. The timber river and dock wall at Victoria Wharf, for example, constructed in 1585, was built as a wharf frontage but fell into disrepair, and then acted only as a river wall with ad hoc front bracing (Tyler 2001). However, the high bank of ooze (or riverine silt) shown in front of the Pacific Wharf site on the Collins map of 1684 (Fig 7) must eventually have rendered the frontage useless as a wharf.

Compared with other excavated examples of 17th-century timber river frontages, Waterfront 1 was reasonably carefully

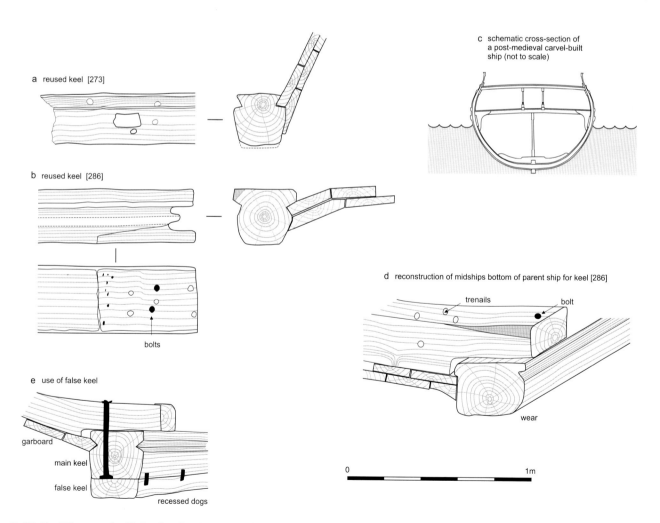

Fig 37 *The 17th-century ships' keel timbers, [286] and [273], found in Waterfront 1 (a–d) and a late 18th-century false keel found in the trestle foundation of Building 6 (e) (scale 1:20)*

designed, and solidly built by trained carpenters, although expenses were reduced by using much second-hand timber and relatively cheap softwood. The rebuilding of the frontage at its eastern end entailed the use of second-hand, oak carvel-ship planking as sheathing, spiked to the riverward side of assorted, clearly reused, oak piles.

The reused ship timbers from Waterfront 1

Some of the most informative reused ship timbers incorporated in Waterfront 1 were two large sections of oak keels, [286] and [273], that were used as the main beams of land-tie assemblies. They were both altered slightly for reuse, by cutting large rectangular sockets with augers, chisels and axes for the oak lock-bars that wedged against the anchor stakes, but their original form remains clear. They were of similar form and size and may well have been taken from the same vessel (Fig 37).

The keel was the foundation or backbone of a ship. Into it was hewn and carved a watertight rebate, or rabbet, for the first course of lower planking (the garboard strakes) on either side of the hull. The cross-section of the longer section of keel ([286], Fig 37b and d) shows that it was derived from the less-sharply rising part of the middle of the parent ship. The similar but slightly narrower keel section ([273], Fig 37a) had rabbets cut to fit steeply-rising garboard strakes such as would have been found at the ends of the vessel. At the ends of many vessels, the keel was often made narrower (the siding was reduced). Although we do not have any well-recorded English examples to compare the Pacific Wharf keel timbers with, we do have information from some contract documents, including that for keel repairs to HMS Dartmouth and other naval vessels (Martin 1978, 55; Goodwin 1987, 231). In these two documents of the 1670s, keels of medium-sized warships, called frigates, were specified at 13 inches and 15 inches (325mm and 375mm) square. We have no evidence that the keel sections from Pacific Wharf were derived from a naval vessel (or vessels), and they may well have come from a merchant ship (or ships) that was possibly built more lightly. However, we can suggest that the keel timbers probably came from a medium-sized deep sea vessel measuring in the region of 75–110 feet (22–33m) on the keel, which would translate into a vessel with a hull of approximately 30–41m in length. The width or beam of the vessel would have been approximately 8–10m.

Dendrochronology has provided a felling date range of 1621–57 for keel timber [273] (Tyers 2000). The artefactual evidence implies that Waterfront 1 was built in the 1650s or early 1660s. Since both keels were worn, it is likely that they came from a vessel or vessels built in the period 1621– c 1650.

Specific features of the keel timbers

Keel section [286] was in excess of 11.6m long. It ended in a horizontal stopped splayed scarf joint, for joining it to a section of the keel that led forward in the parent vessel. At its widest it was sided 375mm (15 inches) and it had a worn depth or moulding of c 280mm, which must have been deeper when

the timber was new. The end of the scarf had been fastened with a mixture of c 34mm diameter oak treenails and iron spikes. Two c 30mm diameter bolt holes were also found. The overall length of the scarf was probably over 1.3m, and it may even have been hooked or tabled. It is likely therefore that keel timber [286] was over 12m long.

Keel section [273] was truncated by later activity but had a siding of c 300mm and a worn depth of 270mm. This timber, together with the others dated by dendrochronology, came from south-east England, probably Kent or the lower Thames valley (I Tyers, pers comm).

The size of the rebates implied a thickness of the garboards of c 50mm (two inches), which is surprisingly thin for a medium-sized ship. However, staining on the sides of both keels clearly showed that the parent vessel(s) had two layers of hull planking, almost certainly from new. In the case of keel section [273], traces of iron spikes, with square shanks c 8mm across, showed that this second layer of hull planking was nailed over the first (Fig 37a). The use of double carvel planking is known from several ships of the late 16th and 17th centuries found in continental Europe (eg Lemee 1997, 52). It does not appear to have been common (judging from documentary sources) in English naval craft, although it may have been more common in merchant vessels. The use of timber from south-east England for keel section [273] implies therefore that the vessel was built locally using an uncommon technique. The use of two layers of planking is not to be confused with the use of sacrificial sheathing of thin softwood boards sometimes used on English vessels at that time (Martin 1978, 49).

On keel section [286], a sliver of sawn-oak garboard planking remained attached. It was 45–50mm thick and had a stop splayed or nibbed scarf in it about 420mm long. Traces of tarred plant-fibre waterproofing, or luting, were found in the keel rabbet and analysis has shown it to be oakum made from hemp (Cannabis sativa L). Oakum was frequently used as a waterproofing material in carvel-built vessels and it is a common misconception that it was usually made from hemp, based on the mistaken view that rope was usually made from that fibre. Other samples of caulking fibres (from dumped deposits associated with the construction of Waterfronts 1, 2 and 4) have been identified as goat hair, which is the waterproofing material found most frequently on post-medieval sites in Southwark (Walton Rogers 2002, 2). The sample from the keel rabbet is believed to be the first confidently identified example in Britain, of oakum that is genuinely made from hemp (Walton Rogers 2002, 3)

Faint traces of cream-coloured deposits were found on both keels. This may have been a type of under water paint such as white lead or graves – a mixture of tallow, resin and sometimes brimstone (Abell 1948, 91).

The first layer of hull planking was fastened to the keel in the rabbet with 25mm shaved oak treenails, which did not appear to have been locked with wedges inboard. These fastenings were set at 300–350mm centres and must have been carefully made, with slightly expanded heads to draw in the planks tight. Once driven, they must have been cut back with a saw and adze to be flush before the second layer of planking was fitted.

On the upper faces of the keel timbers (as they would have been in the parent ships) were obvious impressions of the lowest framing timbers; the floors. These were c 230mm wide (sided) and they had clearly been bolted to the keel with 25mm diameter round-shanked iron bolts of some kind (Fig 37b). The pattern of the holes suggests that every floor was bolted in the mid-ships whilst only alternate floors were bolted at the ends. Interestingly, there was no evidence at all for the fitting of a false keel on either keel section. Although common on naval ships, they were not always used on merchant vessels (Lemee 1997, 32).

A glimpse of early 17th-century trees used by shipwrights

The keel of a vessel was usually made up from the longest timber available within the budget of the project, and it is clear that most of the length of the original timber was found in keel section [286], which measured in excess of 11.6m. Although it was not possible to examine all the surfaces of the timber *in situ* it was apparent that the parent tree for this keel section was tall and straight, without large boughs for most of that length. The keel was hewn out neatly with no very clear axe or adze marks surviving, but the limit of the tree was used and occasionally a little sapwood was left in places.

We can reconstruct the parent log as about 0.55m diameter at the mid length, or perhaps 0.75m diameter at breast height. The tree-ring study shows that the parent tree was fairly slow grown and perhaps around 120–150 years old (Tyers 2000). A tree of this size and shape must have grown in amongst other tall trees to prevent large branches developing, and oaks such as this appear to have been rare in England in the post-medieval period. In fact, studies are showing that during that period, English trees were typically rather fast grown and squatter in form, rarely providing timber over 8.0m long (eg Saxby and Goodburn 1998, 182). Indeed, no tree-ring match for this particular timber has been identified and it might even have been of foreign origin.

The smaller section of keel [273] was cut from a tree of medium growth rate with a slightly smaller diameter, being approximately 90–120 years old when it was felled. This is much more characteristic of post-medieval English timber and this example appears to have come from Kent or the Thames valley (I Tyers, pers comm).

The reused ship's pump elements

The development of ship's pumps

After the sails and steering gear, anchors and pumps were the crucial pieces of equipment in large sea-going vessels, and remains of both have been found at the Pacific Wharf site. It is hard for us now to understand how important reliable pumps were for the crews, passengers and cargoes of large, wooden sailing vessels; their efficacy was sometimes a matter of life and death (Oertling 1996). Pumps were also used on land to raise well water and to drain underground workings, and it is fair to note

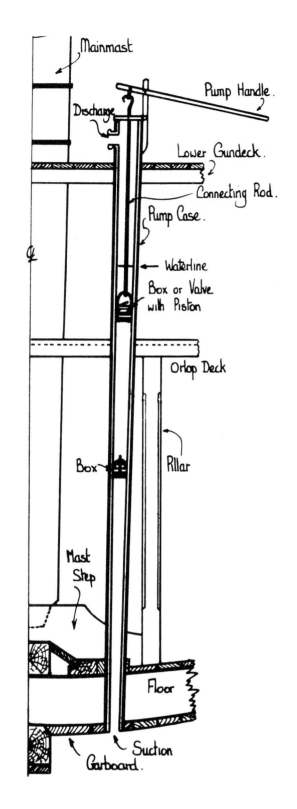

Fig 38 (above and facing) *Two types of ship's pumps c 1780: a – elm log pump, for deck washing and fire fighting; b – chain bilge pump (Goodwin 1987 figs 5/14, 5/9)*

that their development was linked intrinsically to the development of steam power and industrial machines in the 18th century.

It should also be noted that large 18th-century ships would usually have had two types of pump. They had one for lifting clean seawater to wash down the ship and to prevent the upper hull and decks from drying out too much in hot conditions, and also for fire fighting. There would also be one or (more

b

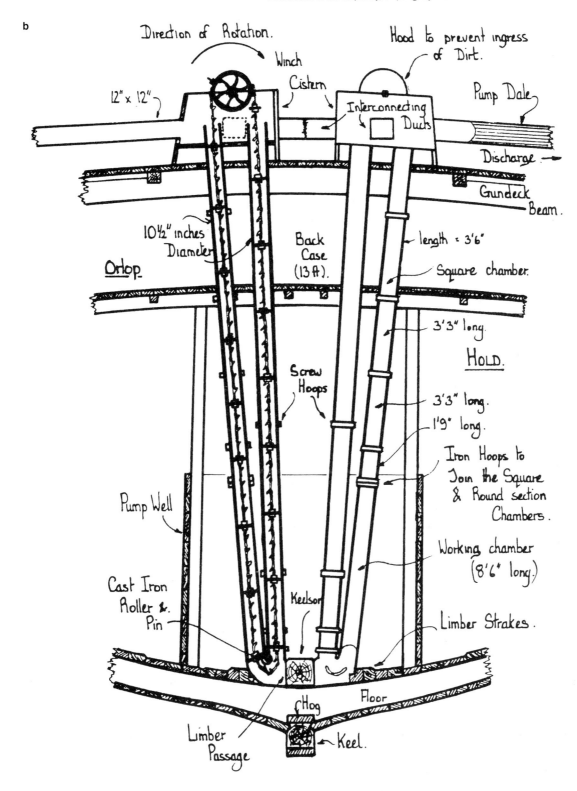

Direction of Rotation.

Hood to prevent ingress of Dirt.

Winch

Cistern

Pump Dale

12" x 12"

Interconnecting Ducts

Discharge

Gundeck Beam.

10½" inches Diameter

Back Case (13 ft).

length = 3'6"

Orlop

Square chamber.

3'3" long.

HOLD.

Screw Hoops

3'3" long.

1'9" long.

Iron Hoops to Join the Square & Round section Chambers.

Pump Well

Working chamber (8'6" long.)

Cast Iron Roller & Pin

Keelson

Limber Strakes.

Hog

Floor

Limber Passage

Keel.

usually) a pair of bilge pumps, used to expel water that leaked or ran into the vessel.

The simplest type of pump, used from at least late medieval times, was built from one or more bored log tubes. It was fitted with a non-return valve about half way down, and a wooden piston with a valve linked to a rod and lever (Fig 38a). In the 17th century, the chain pump was developed, and this type continued in use (particularly for bilge pumps) through the 18th century (Goodwin 1987, 138). Here, a series of metal-backed leather disks were pulled up and down two linked pipes on a continuous metal chain, by crew members winding handles linked to a drive wheel (Fig 38b).

Clearly, both types of pump required some form of pipe and this could be made in a number of different ways

(Oertling 1996, 13–14). The most common early form was a simple bored log or squared baulk. A pipe could also be made by sawing a baulk lengthwise down the middle, hollowing it out and then rejoining the halves. This method is known from at least the late 1680s, and a much later example was found at the Pacific Wharf site (Chapter 2.5, period 5, S17). Tubes could also be made out of staves, or even in square section out of planks, although these were not the usual methods.

Early accounts of pump pipe making have been drawn together by Oertling, and Edlin and others have recorded the English 19th-century tradition of such work (Oertling 1996, 10–14; Edlin 1949, 57–8). The making of bored wooden pipes was a specialised craft, requiring a large set of augers and reamers and a very long turning bar fitted with a long cross handle. Logs to be used might have been simply debarked, de-limbed and bucked to length, or they might have been hewn to a square shape, after marking the desired bore centres on the log ends. The timber was always worked green, when it was softer. The sections of pipe were held securely on blocks or a frame, and the boring begun. At first small bits would have been used, then larger, tapered reamers. In order to overcome the problem of drilling such long holes, the auger (or wimble) bar had to be laid on a rest of timber to support its weight and to help guide it. This may have given rise to its name, 'restwymball' (Edlin 1949, 56).

A 17th-century ship's pump (S2)

A drain (S2), associated with the use of Waterfront 2 in period 2 (Chapter 2.2), was clearly constructed from reused pipe elements of a ship's pump (Fig 39). It was made in at least four interlocking sections, three of which survived in situ. Each junction was made in the same way as the more typical elm log water pipes, in which a long, neatly tapered 'male' end was driven snugly into the 'female' end of the neighbouring section of pipe. Thus the opening at the non-tapered end of the pipe was larger than the actual bore. This is an unusual find: although the remains of some ship's pump bases are known from shipwreck excavations, large lengths of piping are rarely found.

It has been suggested that in Europe elm was the most popular species group for pump pipes but that larch, beech and alder were also used (Oertling 1996, 10). Elm is the species found most commonly for post-medieval bored-log water pipes in London, and it was used for rural pump making in England until the turn of the 20th century. In the 18th century, elm and pine were used in Scotland for making pipes and they were sometimes exported to London (Edlin 1949, 56). Elm (in all its species and sub-species) was reputedly used for pipe making because it is durable when wet, but in practice the timber in a ship's pump would have been wet and dry in service. The key feature in favour of elm might have been its resistance to splitting and wear in use.

The northern section of the composite drain was indeed made of the preferred elm, but the adjoining section was (very surprisingly) made of oak that had been treated in the same

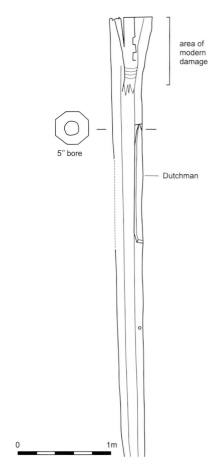

Fig 39 *An oak section from a ship's pump reused as part of a drain (S2) (scale 1:40)*

way. The length of this section of pipe was c 5.8m with the southern (male) end partly hidden in the next section to the south. The bore was slightly off centre leaving the sides rather thin; they had split in one area and a small oak patch bedded in tarred hair was nailed over the split (a repair known as a Dutchman). The bore was c 125mm (five inches) with a tapered opening at the north end reaching c 190mm diameter. The diameter of the upper pipe of a typical farm water pump at the end of the 19th century was apparently five inches, whilst that of the lower pipe was commonly two inches (Edlin 1949, 57). This arrangement allowed the piston in the upper bore to lift more water with less travel, as the lever at the top could not travel far with each stroke. It is possible therefore that the oak pump section was an upper element of a ship's pump.

The pump sections had been first accurately hewn square following marked guidelines, then hewn to an eight-sided cross section. This would have been particularly important in the oak section, to remove as much as possible of the weak, rot-prone sapwood. Clearly the bore wandered a little in making the oak section leaving it far from central, but it had obviously been good enough to be used on a ship before its final use as a simple drain pipe.

Ship's pump making in the 19th century

In the 19th century, an unusual form of timber gutter or drain with a loose, plank lid (Chapter 2.5, period 5, S17) was laid in the ship-breaking yard (OA5). The feature of interest here is that the lower part of the assembly was built of carefully made sections of large, ship's pump pipe timbers (Fig 40). The well-preserved timbers were made of dense tropical hardwood. Each element had been hewn and planed on the outside with a slight taper and neatly hollowed on the inside to make half the pipe. The mating faces were alternately tongued and grooved so as to make a watertight fit. Rust staining showed clearly how the halves of each section had then been bound with iron hoops set about 0.6m (two feet) apart. Where connections were made, the pipes had male and female tapers and at one point, the join had been repaired with a thin lead sheet (Fig 33; Fig 40). The bore of the pipe was 200mm (eight inches), which is big enough to suggest that the pump pipes had been part of a chain pump assembly rather than a simple piston arrangement.

The outside of each half had a very neatly chiselled and plough-planed groove of unknown function; some small iron nail shanks were found in places on either side of the groove. As it is probable that this pump was a product of the early industrial age, perhaps this groove was used to key the timber to a bed that could then pass a water-, horse- or steam-powered rotary cutter. The industrial production of bored log pumps of pine for the London market was in progress at least as early as 1770 (Edlin 1949, 126). If, as has been suggested, making pump pipes in two halves was originally a Spanish tradition of

work, it was clearly copied by north Europeans on occasion (Oertling 1996, 14). This example, made from tropical hardwood, may have been taken from a ship built in the Far East or elsewhere.

Reconstructing 18th- and 19th-century cranes

In the working of a large ship-building, repair or breaking yard, one or more cranes were essential, for loading and unloading the timbers (some weighing well over a tonne) that would have been coming in and going out of the yard by land or water. Temporary sheer-leg lifting devices would have been used for the same purpose. The excavation at Pacific Wharf has produced evidence for some possible crane bases dating to the periods when the site was used for shipbuilding (S11–S13, period 4) and ship breaking (S15, period 5).

What would these cranes have looked like? Perhaps our best sources here are panoramic Thames-side paintings. One of these, by John Cleveley the Elder, shows a large weather-boarded wheel crane used for unloading a timber barge at Deptford Naval Dockyard in 1752 (Fig 13). The maritime artist and shipwright James Dodds has redrawn one of these post-medieval wheel cranes to show its structure and bracing foundations (Dodds and Moore 1984, fig 22; Fig 41). Dodds' illustration has some similarities to the 19th-century crane base (Chapter 2.5, S15, period 5) at the Pacific Wharf site, although here the assembly was partially below the contemporary ground surface.

The trestle foundation of Building 6

Introduction

The most unusual and enigmatic timber structure found at the Pacific Wharf site was the trestle foundation for Building 6, period 5 (Chapter 2.5). Although superficially the individual trestles resembled the probable crane bases (S11–S13, period 4) that they superseded, it seems likely that the foundation supported a substantial raised floor of a large timber building, possibly open-sided (Fig 30; Fig 42).

The trestles were built solidly but cheaply; perhaps they represented a cheaper alternative to a driven pile foundation, as no piling rig and gang were needed and a carpenter with perhaps two labourers could have built the whole structure. Another factor might have been lack of space to rig a pile driver on that part of the site, perhaps because of an existing overhanging roof for a building that has otherwise left no trace in the archaeological record.

Aspects of the carpentry of the trestle foundation of Building 6

The structure was clearly built by woodworkers with some knowledge of making timber frames such as trestles and roof trusses. For comparison, the carpentry in the 18th-century buildings at Chatham dockyard has two main styles, suggesting

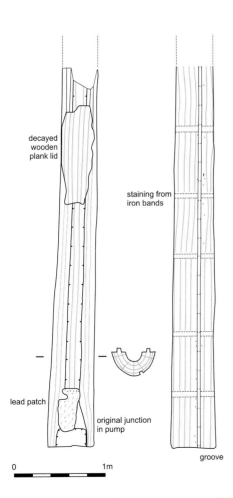

decayed wooden plank lid

staining from iron bands

lead patch

original junction in pump

groove

0   1m

Fig 40 Part of a tropical-hardwood ship's pump reused in a gutter/drain (S17) (scale 1:40)

Fig 41 *Reconstruction drawing of an 18th-century wheel crane, similar to Structure 15, period 5; note the flat-bottomed timber-laden barges resting on the foreshore and the absence of front bracing to the river wall (Dodds and Moore 1984, fig 22) (© James Dodds)*

that some were built by carpenters, using typical carpentry tools and materials, and others by shipwrights, using some techniques common in shipwrightry but not carpentry. This set of trestles has some similarities with the 18th-century carpentry noted at Chatham. These include the use of second-hand ship's timbers, the use of joints cut to fairly wide tolerances and the use of face nailing for the heads of the braces (Fig 43). These were simplifications compared to the typical timber framing of the 17th century, as employed in the construction of Waterfront 1. The very late 18th-century carpentry of the dry dock bases, altars and sides found at West India Docks (London) was by contrast made entirely from new, imported pine, and extensive use was made of iron bolts and spikes and lap joints (Pitt and Goodburn in prep).

Although their work was simple and a little rough in execution, the woodworkers had gone to the trouble of providing some of the upright posts with pegged stub tenons, but the pegs were not used in the final construction. This was

probably because the trench in which the trestles were constructed was so narrow that there was not space to drive the pegs.

The second-hand ship timbers used in the trestle foundation of Building 6

The ship timbers reused in the trestles were derived from vessels built in the late 18th century, and can be grouped into three main categories. The sill beams were nearly all made from sections of false keels, the diagonal braces were framing timbers that had mostly been resawn lengthways and the vertical posts were reused deck beams.

With one exception, the trestle sill beams were made from lengths of second-hand false keels. These were sacrificial beams placed under the main keel of the ship to take wear and protect it from damage (see Fig 37e). The idea was that in the event of the ship running aground the false keel could be torn off without damaging the main structural keel. The increase in

Fig 42 *One of the trestles forming the foundation of Building 6, from the west*

depth of the keel projection also helped to improve sailing into the wind by reducing leeway.

This category of ship timber has not been found before in London excavations, despite the fact that they must often have been replaced in Thames-side shipyards. After the main keel bolts had been driven, the false keel beams were fastened by means of relatively weak iron dogs (large staples) 20mm wide. These were housed in recesses in the sides of the timbers to protect them and reduce drag (Fig 43a). Not all keels were extended in this way (for example, the 17th-century keels reused as land-ties in Waterfront 1) but it was common on all but the smallest naval vessels.

By 1719 the naval Establishment List, describing standardised scantlings of warship elements, refers to large ships of 50–70 guns being fitted with false keels four inches thick (Goodwin 1987, 244). This dimension corresponds to the examples of false keels found at the Pacific Wharf site, which were 100mm (four inches) thick and c 280mm wide.

In the 18th century, some ships, such as HMS *Victory*, had two false keels. The materials for 18th-century false keels were usually elm or beech, both tough timbers, but cheaper than the oak used for the main keel. At the Pacific Wharf site, one false keel section was of beech (with some race-cut markings, possibly merchants' marks, on its upper surface) while the others were of elm.

The one sill beam (from B6) that did not originate from a ship's false keel was a hewn softwood beam, with traces of cream paint and several redundant nail holes, and was probably of building origin (Fig 43b).

The diagonal braces were mostly made from ship's oak framing timbers that had been resawn longitudinally. Fresh marks of pit-sawing could be seen on many of the faces, whilst in other cases the timbers bore the undulating surfaces left by axe and adze hewing. Shaved oak treenails were the principal fastening used in the frames of English-built vessels in the late 17th and 18th centuries, and this meant that frame timbers and planking could easily be resawn for secondary use.

The reconstructed sizes of frame timbers halved by sawing would have been c 280–320mm wide (or sided) with varying depths (or mouldings) of c 180–280mm. These are the scantlings of large, sea-going ships. It is not possible to be more specific as the sizes of framing timbers varied with the position away from the keel, so that there was an overlap in the sizes of framing timbers between vessels of markedly different overall dimensions.

The sizes of the oak treenails varied in each frame timber, with the overall range including treenails of 34mm, 38mm and 42mm diameters. These sizes imply an origin in large ships rather than small ships or boats. It is impossible to be more precise than this, despite the existence of documented

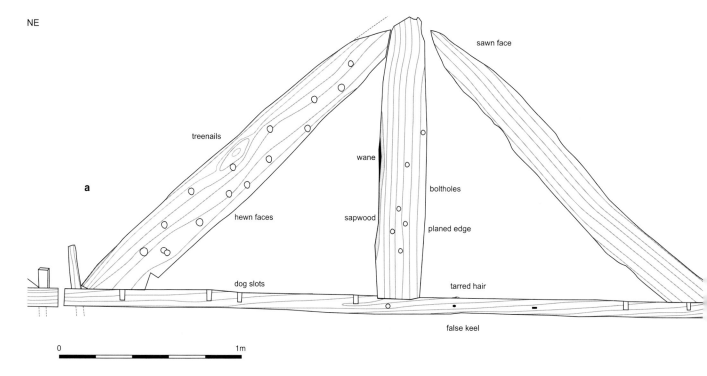

NE

sawn face

treenails

wane

boltholes

a

planed edge

hewn faces

sapwood

dog slots

tarred hair

false keel

0   1m

Fig 43 *Two trestle assemblies from the foundation of Building 6 showing details of construction and the use of second-hand ship's timbers: a – trestle with a plain deck beam used as the post and a false-keel timber used as the sill beam; b – trestle with a moulded deck beam used as the post and a softwood building timber used as the sill beam (scale 1:20)*

'rules of thumb' relating ship size and treenail size, such as one inch for every 100 feet, with a 74 gun ship like HMS *Valiant* having one-and-a-half inch (38mm) treenails (Lavery 1991, 69–70). The making of treenails for ship, barge and boat building along the Thames was a specialised craft, with large yards (such as that at Blackwall) and naval facilities having their own treenail makers, even as late as the mid 19th century (Dodd 1843, 467).

The treenails in the reused framing timbers were all of oak with 8 or 16 shaved sides; they were not made completely round. They were fashioned of medium- or fast-grown, tough oak rather than weaker, slow-grown material that would have been easier to carve. It appears that very fast-grown, old, oak, coppiced stems or timber of like quality were preferred for this work by the end of the 18th century (Steel 1997, 437). The logs to be used were cut to various lengths up to four feet (1.3m) and split into billets, resulting in treenails that were stronger than if they had been sawn out. The rough billets were then trimmed to a square section with a keen hatchet, probably with its blade bevelled on one side only for greater accuracy. The trimmed billet was then 8- or 16-sided using a form of draw knife (S Rankin, pers comm). In 1843, Dodd illustrated this process, based on observation of the work of treenail makers in a Blackwall shipyard, and it is clear that the knife was used with a pushing action whilst the billet remained wedged between the worker's body and a notched support (Fig 44).

The ends of the treenails were usually left square or at least larger than the shank, to act as a head to draw in the planking. The head was then cut off flush with the planking and was usually split and expanded so as to lock tight and not leak. The inboard ends of treenails were then sawn off, split and usually

wedged to lock in the same manner as a rivet; very different from a carpenter's peg. The sawn off blunt points and heads of treenails are indicative of ship building or repair and have been found at a number of post-medieval waterfront sites in London (Goodburn in prep).

All the framing timbers were cut from slightly or moderately curved oak logs (Fig 34) that showed a small amount of sapwood and (occasionally) wane in places. The parent logs would have been in the region of 40–50mm in diameter and many of them were a little knotty. It is likely that they came from the upper parts of rather open-grown oaks, perhaps derived from pasture land or hedgerows.

The hewn surfaces of some of the timbers were moderately well preserved and bore some axe stop marks from the initial siding, or roughing out of the straight sides. The largest stop mark was 130mm long and not complete, indicating that the axes used had blades of perhaps 140–150mm width. The most common tool marks on the surfaces of the timbers were the characteristic dimples left by an adze used across the grain. However, as these tools were used in the final smoothing and trimming of the frames (the dubbing) the blades were not allowed to bite in deeply. Thus the widest stop marks were very incomplete at 70mm and it is likely that the adze blades were actually at least 100mm wide.

The craft of hewing structural timbers seems to have died out by the middle of the 19th century in England. Dodd does not mention seeing it, for example, at Thames-side shipyards in the 1840s, when the siding of timber and even the initial cutting of the curved edges was carried out over the saw pit rather than by hewing. It is clear, however, that the frame

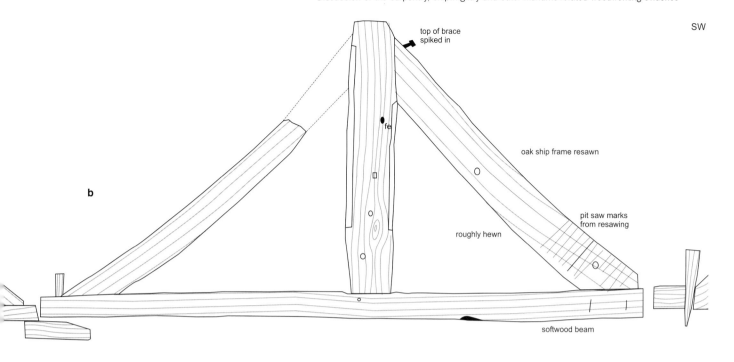

b

top of brace
spiked in

fe

oak ship frame resawn

pit saw marks
from resawing

roughly hewn

softwood beam

Fig 44 *The art of treenail making*
in a Thames shipyard (Dodd 1843,
467 fig 3)

timbers used in the foundation of Building 6 were made by the process of hewing with axes and trimming and smoothing with adzes. According to Steel, this method was still considered an alternative to pit-sawing as late as 1818 (Steel 1818, 2).

Boxed-heart, oak deck beams were reused as the vertical posts of the trestles, presumably because they were substantial timbers with straight, parallel sides. The scantlings varied but they were typically c 250m x 280mm, which shows that they came from medium-sized to large ships. Unfortunately, the scantling of deck beams varied from deck to deck in a large vessel, with those of the upper deck being smaller and comparable in size to those used in quite small vessels. However, a number of diagnostic features show clearly that the deck beams used here were derived from large craft:

1) they all had sides with few fastenings, although one beam had a housing for a carline;

2) they all had one face marked with nail holes from fastening the decking;

3) they all had up to four 25mm (one inch) diameter bolt holes for fastenings to hanging knees;

4) they all had a chamfer or moulding on the two lower corners, opposite the face with deck nails in. This was done to strengthen the edge of the beam, remove most of any remaining sapwood and reduce the risk of head injury in the often relatively low headroom between decks.

The beams were all neatly finished and planed, making it impossible to tell how they had been converted. Those with mouldings on what would have been the lower corners in the ship probably came from the officers' end of the vessel, which was usually more embellished. Faint traces of white paint of some kind were also found on some of the beams.

The construction of late 18th- to early 19th-century ships' anchors

No direct parallel for the complex anchor stock reused in Structure 15, period 4 (Fig 32) can be found (see Curryer 1999). However, there are some illustrations of composite anchors with two iron flukes and a shank in one piece, clasped by a two-piece timber stock. The type is called the 'Admiralty long-shank' anchor, as illustrated in Steel's *The elements and practice of rigging and seamanship* (1794) (Fig 32). The halves of the stock were made from a fast-grown softwood, possibly a pine. They had been held together with oak treenails of 34mm diameter and then bound by at least two iron bands, indicated by rust staining. In the middle, where they would have clasped the iron shank of the anchor, two intricately worked elm inserts were fitted and nailed in, presumably because the elm would have been more resistant to wear. An anchor with a stock this size would have belonged to a large sea-going vessel.

4

Conclusions

4.1 Development of the site

The archaeological investigation at Pacific Wharf has revealed the post-medieval development of a part of the Rotherhithe waterfront in considerable detail and produced a wealth of data relating to the maritime industries that operated there. By relating the results of the fieldwork to cartographic and documentary evidence, it has been possible to consider the development of the site in the broader context of post-medieval settlement and land use in Rotherhithe. The discovery and analysis of ship's timbers, reused extensively in the construction of river walls, waterfront buildings and other structures such as crane bases, has provided a number of valuable insights into post-medieval shipbuilding technology.

It has been shown for the first time that the development of this stretch of the Thames waterfront was hampered by the nature of the local topography. Due to a localised anomaly in the natural strata, the riverbank was indented here and the area was particularly low-lying and susceptible to flooding, unsuitable conditions for occupation, until the construction of the first timber river wall (Waterfront 1) in the middle of the 17th century.

In the 1660s, the site formed part of Sir William Warren's timber yard, and it is quite likely that he was responsible for the construction, or at least the subsequent maintenance, of Waterfront 1. By the 1680s, this part of Warren's yard was leased to a member of the Shorter family, who was probably also engaged in the timber trade. The method of construction of Waterfront 1 (notably the absence of front bracing) is consistent with the use of the waterfront as a timber wharf where vessels of shallow draft could moor, to receive or unload materials.

During the second half of the 18th century, the Woolcombe family of shipbuilders occupied the site. They were probably responsible for enlarging the site, by the construction of Waterfront 4, and for constructing the wet dock, Structure 6. At their Bull Head yard, the Woolcombes built a number of relatively small vessels for the use of the Royal Navy, as well as merchant vessels for which no records survive. By that time, few warships were being built in the Lower Pool, and this presaged the decline of shipbuilding that was to affect the whole of the Rotherhithe waterfront in the following century. The archaeological evidence for this period indicates that most of the site was an open yard, perhaps for timber storage or for carrying out woodworking tasks associated with the repair of vessels moored in the wet dock.

In the early 19th century, the Beatson family acquired the Pacific Wharf site for use as a ship-breaking and repair yard, and for their trade in imported timber. This was typical of developments at many Rotherhithe shipyards at that time (particularly this far upstream) when, for many reasons, shipbuilding had started to become unprofitable. The Beatsons invested considerable capital, breathing new life into the site. For example, they constructed new warehouses (including B5), and a family house (B6) in the best contemporary style. The site continued in use as a shipyard until the 1870s, but by then it had, like most of the Rotherhithe yards, became uneconomic for that purpose.

4.2 Woodworking evidence

The excavation and study of the 17th- and 18th-century woodworking evidence has highlighted innovations in waterfront carpentry techniques that were quite distinct from those of the late medieval period in London. Clear trends towards labour-saving techniques and materials are demonstrated by the more widespread application of wrought-iron fastenings for land-tie assemblies and by the use of imported softwood timber.

The selective detailed investigation of reused 17th- and 18th-century ship timbers has clarified several aspects of shipwrightry and specialised ancillary trades. The site has provided insights into the making of keels and false keels that have not been produced by other ship discoveries made on land or underwater in Britain. Some surprising new information on the making of ship's pumps and anchors has also been revealed.

4.3 Post-medieval river levels

The problem of rising sea level, as a result of isostatic change and the effects of global warming, is of real concern today, and information from waterfront excavations is vital for understanding this process. The postulated height of c +3.0m OD for Waterfront 1 suggests that, by the mid 17th century, mean high water spring tides in the Lower Pool of the Thames were reaching to about that level. For comparison, during much of the late medieval period, mean high water spring tidal level was at c +2.2–2.5m OD (Goodburn in prep), while the present day (1970s) level at London Bridge is at +3.9m OD (Chapter 2.1, Period 1:discussion). The evidence from Pacific Wharf forms part of a growing body of data relating to river levels during the post-medieval period.

The steady increase in the yard surfaces of the wharfs and working areas, from c +3.0m OD in 1660 to over +4.0m OD by the early 20th century, is clear. The suggested increase in high spring tide levels has thus been c 0.3m per century since 1660.

FRENCH AND GERMAN SUMMARIES

Résumé

Ce volume présente les résultats d'une fouille archéologique entreprise à Pacific Wharf, 165 Rotherhithe Strreet, Londres SE 16, sur la rive sud de la Tamise. Cette fouille a été étroitement liée à une étude historique ce qui a donné beaucoup de détails sur le développement d'une partie des quais donnant sur la rivière à Rotherhithe à l'époque post-médiévale et a produit énormément de données sur les industries maritimes qui y prenaient place.

Les couches géologiques du site étaient les couches de Woolwich et Reading recouvertes par des apports de graviers de la plaine alluviale du Pléistocène. Les variations de niveaux des couches du Pléistocène sur ce site et sur ceux aux alentours indiquent que Pacific Wharf est situé au sud ouest d'une importante dépression qui est peut-être ce qui reste d'un affluent de la Tamise. Des couches alluviales épaisses recouvrant les graviers de la plaine alluviale du Pléistocène se sont accumulées dans cette dépression naturelle quand ce lieu était situé dans la zone des marées de la Tamise et était souvent inondé.

Au milieu du 17ème siècle un quai en bois fut construit le long de la rivière et a permis que, pour la première fois, ce terrain marginal qui était auparavant très bas ait pu être occupé d'une façon permanente. Des données cartographiques suggèrent que, à cette époque, le site faisait partie du grand chantier de bois de Sir William Warren et que, pendant les années 1680, il était occupé par un membre de la famille Shorter, une famille de marchands de bois. La forme du quai le long de la rivière (qui était concu pour permettre aux navires à petit tirage de s'amarrer le long du site) confirme que le site a été développé comme débarcadère commercial et avait probablement un lien avec le commerce du bois. Peu après la construction du premier quai on y fit des réparations importantes probablement parce que la structure s'était effondrée en partie. Avant la fin du 17ème siècle, l'envasement du premier quai a réduit sa viabilité et un autre quai fut construit à environ un mètre de la structure d'origine.

Au début du 18ème siècle, le site fut encore aggrandi par la construction d'un autre quai en bois de bonne taille à environ 5.0m en avant du deuxième quai. Ceci améliora sans doute l'accès au site en provenance de la rivière en créant une plus grande profondeur d'eau tout près du site. Les données archéologiques, cartographiques et documentaires sur l'usage du site à cette époque ne sont pas très précises mais il est probable qu'il a continué à être un quai commercial.

Pendant la première partie du 18ème siècle, le site fut occupé par la famille Woolcombe, une famille de constructeurs de navires qui en entreprit un réaménagement important. Le front de la rivière fut avancé par plus de 40m grâce à la construction d'un nouveau quai et un bassin à flot fut construit derrière ce quai. On éleva le niveau du sol de tout le site ce qui eut sans doute pour effet de créer un chantier naval qui était à l'abri des inondations et un quai le long duquel des navires à plus grand tirage pouvaient s'amarrer.

Au début du 19ème siècle, la famille Beatson acheta le site et le transforma en chantier de briseurs de navires. On y construisit une maison d'habitation élégante qui donnait sur le bassin et à côté un entrepôt qui s'étendait le long de la rivière.

Un bâtiment en bois de grande taille fut construit au sud du bassin sur des fondations en bois d'un type inhabituel qui n'a pas été relevé archéologiquement avant cette étude. Ce bâtiment a pu servir d'entrepôt ou d'atelier. En 1859, une autre compagnie de briseurs de navires appartenant à William Philip Beech occupa ce site.

A partir de 1873 jusqu'à nos jours ou presque le site fut occupé par une série de propriétaires de quais. Pendant cette période, le quai en bois fut remplacé par un quai en béton et le bassin fut également reconstruit en béton. La maison et l'entrepôt construits par les Beatson furent démolis et remplacés par des locaux commerciaux plus importants.

Les données archéologiques indiquent une série de quais et de structures associées comme par example des bâtiments, canalisations et assises de grues ce qui a des renseignements importants sur les techniques de travail du bois à l'époque post-médiévale. Beaucoup de ces structures comprenaient des éléments de navires réutilisés, tels les bois des carcasses, des quilles, des pompes et une base d'ancre qui illustrent bien des aspects clés de la technologie de la construction des navires.

Les objets que l'on a retrouvés provenaient surtout de décharges associées à la construction des quais des 17ème et 18ème siècles. Ils comprenaient de nombreux rejets de céramique de Delft et des éléments de fours, certains d'entre eux provenaient de l'atelier de poterie de Rotherhithe situé près de là à Platform Wharf. Les données sur l'environnement du site comprenaient surtout des échantillons de matériaux utilisés pour imperméabiliser les bâteaux y compris l'un d'entre eux, le chanvre, qui n'a pas été relevé jusque là dans un contexte archéologique en Grande Bretagne.

Zusammenfassung

Dieser Band beschreibt die Ergebnisse der archäologischen Untersuchungen auf Pacific Wharf, 165 Rotherhithe Street, London SE 16, auf dem Südufer der Themse. In Kombination mit historischen Studien zeigen diese im Detail die nachmittelalterliche Entwicklung eines Teils des Rotherhithe Ufers und liefern eine Fülle von Daten über die Küstenindustrie, die dort arbeitete.

Die unterliegende Geologie dort waren Woolwich und Reading Flöze, überlagert von Treibablagerungen von pleistozenem Flußkies. Die unterschiedliche Tiefe der pleistozenen Ablagerungen hier und auf benachbarten Grabungen deuten darauf hin, daß Pacific Wharf an der Südwestecke einer großen, natürlichen Senke gelegen ist, die möglicherweise der Überrest eines versiegten Nebenflusses ist. Dicke alluviale Ablagerungen, die den pleistozenen Flußkies überlagern, haben sich in dieser natürlichen Senke angesammelt, als die Gegend zur Gezeitenzone der Themse gehörte und Überflutungen ausgesetzt war.

Im 17. Jahrhundert baute man eine hölzerne Flußmauer, die es zum erstenmal erlaubte, das bis dahin niedrig liegende Randgebiet zu besiedeln. Kartographische Unterlagen weisen darauf hin, daß ein Teil der Gegend zu Sir William Warrens ausgedehntem Holzlager gehörte, und daß in den 1680er Jahren ein Mitglied der Holzhändlerfamilie Shorter der Besitzer war. Die Form der Ufermauer war so gestaltet, daß Schiffe mit geringem Tiefgang daran anlegen konnten, was darauf

hinweist, daß die Anlage wahrscheinlich schon als kommerzieller Landungsplatz vermutlich für den Holzhandel geplant war. Sehr bald nach dem Bau der ersten Flußmauer wurden größere Reparaturarbeiten wahrscheinlich als Reaktion auf deren teilweisen Einsturz durchgeführt. Noch vor Ende des 17. Jahrhunderts reduzierte Versandung den Gebrauch des Hafens, so daß eine weitere Flußmauer in etwa 1m Abstand vor die ursprüngliche Konstruktion gesetzt wurde.

Im frühen 18. Jahrhundert wurde der Platz durch den Bau einer stabileren hölzernen Flußmauer, die ungefähr 5m vor der zweiten Uferbefestigung lag, erweitert. Dieses verbesserte den Zugang vom Fluß durch größere Wassertiefe. Archäologische, kartographische und dokumentäre Zeugnisse zur Nutzung der Gegend in jener Zeit sind nicht schlüssig, aber es ist wahrscheinlich, daß die kommerzielle Verwendung fortgesetzt wurde.

In der zweiten Hälfte des 18. Jahrhunderts übernahm die Schiffsbauerfamilie Woolcombe den Platz und unternahm größere Umbauarbeiten. Die Flußfront wurde durch den Bau einer neuen Flußmauer und eines Dockhafens diesseits der Uferbefestigung bis zu 40m vorverlegt. Die Erdoberfläche wurde höhergelegt, sodaß im Ergebnis ein Landeplatz entstand, der sicher vor Überflutung war und an dem Schiffe mit sehr viel größerem Tiefgang anlegen konnten.

Im frühen 19. Jahrhundert erwarb die Beatson-Familie den Platz und baute ihn zu einer Schiffsverwrackung um. Sie errichtete auch ein elegantes Wohngebäude, von dem man einen Blick über den Dockhafen hatte, zusammen mit einem Lagerhaus, das sich bis zum Fluß hinunter erstreckte. Südlich der Dockanlage wurde auf ungewöhnlichen Auflagerfundamenten eines Typs, der bisher noch nicht archäologisch nachgewiesen wurde, ein großes Holzgebäude errichtet. Dieses Gebäude mag als Lagerhalle oder als Werkstatt gedient haben. 1859 arbeitete auf diesem Platz eine andere Schiffsverwrackungsfirma, die William Philip Beech gehörte.

Von 1873 bis fast zum heutigen Tag lebten dort eine Reihe von Kaiaufsehern. Während dieser Zeit wurde die Uferbefestigung durch eine Betonmauer ersetzt und auch die Dockanlage neu in Beton errichtet. Das Haus und die Lagerhalle, die die Familie Beatson errichtet hatten, wurden abgerissen und durch einen größeres kommerzielles Gebäude ersetzt.

Der archäologische Nachweis einer Folge von Flußmauern und dazugehörigen Holzkonstruktionen wie Gebäuden, Drainagen und Kranfundamenten lieferten bedeutende Einblicke in nachmittelalterliche Holzbearbeitungstechniken. Viele der Konstruktionen verwendeten schon benutzte Schiffsteile wie Rahmenhölzer, Kiele, Pumpen und einen Ankerstock, was uns wesentliche Aspekte der Schiffsbautechnologie illustriert.

Die Funde stammten hauptsächlich aus Abfallagen in Verbindung mit den Uferbefestigungen des 17. und 18. Jahrhunderts. Dazu gehören große Mengen von Fehlbränden und Brennofenzubehör, die zum Teil aus der Rotherhithe-Töpferei der nahegelegenen Platform Wharf stammen.

Die organischen Funde aus Erdproben enthielten Dichtungsmaterial, wie es beim Bau von Schiffen verwendet wird, einschließlich einer Art (Hanf), die bisher noch nicht in archäologischem Zusammenhang in Britannien gefunden wurde.

GLOSSARY OF WOODWORKING AND NAUTICAL TERMS

Anchor stakes	Pairs of stakes placed either side of a land-tie beam to retain the lock-bar
Auger	A large drill bit, usually with a fixed handle
Baulk	Log cut to a square or rectangular cross section
Billet	A small, roughly-worked length of timber, used in the manufacture of treenails
Bitt	A strong vertical timber protruding through a vessel's deck, to which other timbers and ropes can be fastened
Box halved	Describes a timber that has been squared from half a log
Boxed heart	Describes a timber that has been squared from a whole log
Box quartered	Describes a timber that has been squared from a quarter log
Bucked	Describes logs that have been cross-cut, often done on a sawbuck
Carline	Fore and aft deck beam element that carried the minor deck beams or ledges
Carvel shipbuilding	Method of building ships where the planking is set edge to edge and fastened to the frames of the hull only, and where the framework is usually set up first
Caulking	Waterproofing material (usually fibres of animal or vegetable origin) that is driven into the gaps between the timbers of a vessel after construction. It is distinct from luting
Conversion	Process of changing rough logs into timbers with flat sides, commonly slabs, planks and beams
Coppiced	Describes a tree that is cut down to the stump and allowed to regrow with multiple stems that can be harvested repeatedly
Dog	Large metal staple use to join timbers
Draw knife	Woodworking tool with a long knife-like blade, usually drawn towards the user whilst shaving wood, often to a rounded cross section
Dubbed	A surface trimmed with an adze
Dutchman	A shallow patch to cover a defect

False keel   Beam set under the main keel of a vessel to protect it and also to improve the vessel's sailing qualities

Floor   The lowest cross-ways frame timber in a vessel's hull

Garboard   The first course of planking (strake) next to the keel in the bottom of a vessel

Hanging knees   Brackets that ran vertically down from the deck beams to hold them to the ship's sides

Hewn   Describes the surface of a timber that has been flattened and shaped with an axe (compare **dubbed**). Also a method of timber conversion

Housing   A joint comprising a recess, usually rectangular, that grips most, or the entire end, of a timber, commonly joining at right angles

Keel   The main central strength member of a vessel's bottom

Land-tie or backbrace   Assembly running landward from a river or dock frontage, designed to resist pressure towards open water

Leeway   The sideways movement of a vessel in the water, caused by the wind

Lock-bar   A timber set cross-ways in a land-tie assembly to lock the main beam to the anchor stakes

Luting   Waterproofing material placed in the joints of a vessel's hull during construction. In historic craft, it is usually a mastic and a fibre. It is distinct from caulking

Mortice   Neatly cut slot for holding a tenon

Moulding   The process of cutting the edges of a ship's timber to a pattern or 'mould', usually curved. Also a dimension from one moulded face to another. In framing, it is the depth dimension

Nibbed scarf   See **stopped splayed scarf**

Oakum   Unpicked rope fibres, commonly used as a waterproofing material in the construction of carvel-built vessels

Pile   A sharpened timber driven into position

Pit-sawing   Method of sawing timber lengthways employing two or more men, with the timber held horizontally over a pit or, less commonly, on a permanent raised frame. Used for the conversion of logs and the resawing of sided timber and baulks

Plate   A horizontal timber beam incorporated into a wall or similar feature, usually as a baseplate or top-plate (see **sill beam**)

Post   Timber set upright in a post-hole or trench, placed on a post-pad or jointed into a sill beam

Rabbet or rebate   A step worked along the edge of a timber

Reamer   Tapered drill bit

Sapwood   The young, perishable wood under the bark of a tree, particularly marked in oak

Scantling   Cross-sectional dimensions of a timber

Scarf   End-to-end joint

Siding   The process of cutting a ship or boat timber to its required thickness. For a frame timber this is in the forward and backward axis of the vessel. Also, a dimension of same. Always carried out before moulding

Sill beam   Timber set horizontally at the base of a wall or similar feature. Often with uprights jointed into it (also baseplate)

Spike   A large nail

Stop mark   Line left when an edged tool stops travelling across a surface. Also known as a 'jam curve'

Stopped splayed scarf   Similar to a through splayed scarf, but with the ends of the timber left blunt and housed below the surface. Known to shipwrights as a nibbed scarf

Strake   A course of planking, usually running the entire length of a vessel

Tenon   Tongue of timber left on the end of a timber to fit in a mortice

Through splayed scarf   Scarf joint in which joining faces are cut away at a slope and the timbers held by the fastenings only

Treenail   Carefully made, cylindrical, wooden peg, used as a watertight fastening in boat and shipbuilding. The ends were often enlarged by splitting and wedging with fibre or wood

Waney   Describes timbers showing traces of the wane, or the irregular surface of the tree under the bark

Wale   Main horizontal timber in a vessel or waterfront wall

Wharfinger   An owner or keeper of a wharf

BIBLIOGRAPHY

Abell, W, 1948 *The shipwright's trade*, Cambridge

Adams, J, in prep *Report on excavations at Bucklers Hard, Hampshire*, Centre for Maritime Archaeology, University of Southampton

Atkinson, D, and Oswald, A, 1969 London clay tobacco pipes *J Brit Archaeol Ass* 32, 171–227

Ayre, J, and Wroe-Brown, R, 2002 *The London Millennium Bridge: excavation of the medieval and later waterfronts at Peter's Hill, City of London, and Bankside, Southwark*, MoLAS Archaeol Stud Ser 6, London

Banbury, P, 1971 *Shipbuilders of the Thames and Medway*, Newton Abbott

Bates, J, 1996 An archaeological field evaluation at Bull Head Wharf, Rotherhithe Street, SE16, London Borough of Southwark, unpub MoL rep

Blatherwick, S, 1999 Tunnel Wharf redevelopment, 121–123 Rotherhithe Street, London SE16: an archaeological assessment, unpub MoL rep

British Geological Survey, 1993 *North London, England and Wales: Sheet 256, solid and drift geology*, 1:50,000, Nottingham

Courtney, T, 1973 Excavations at the Royal Dockyard Woolwich, 1972, *Trans Greenwich and Lewisham Antiq Soc* 8.1, 17–31

Courtney, T, 1974 Excavations at the Royal Dockyard Woolwich, 1973, *Trans Greenwich and Lewisham Antiq Soc* 8.2, 52–60

Cowan, C, 1998 165 Rotherhithe Street, London SE16: an archaeological assessment, unpub MoL rep

Curryer, B, 1999 *Anchors: an illustrated history*, London

Davis, R, 1962 *The rise of the English shipping industry in the 17th and 18th centuries*, London

Divers, D, in prep Excavations at Deptford on the site of the East India Company dockyards and the Trinity House almshouses, London, *Post-medieval Archaeol*

Dodd, G, 1843 *Days at the factories: or, the manufacturing industry of Great Britain described, and illustrated by numerous engravings of machines and processes*, London

Dodds, J, and Moore, J, 1984 *Building the wooden fighting ship*, London

Douglas-Irvine, H, 1912 Rotherhithe, in *The Victoria History of the county of Surrey: Vol 4* (ed H E Malden), 83–92, London

Dugdale, W, 1825 *Monasticon anglicanum* 5, London

Edlin, H, 1949 *Woodland crafts in England*, London

English Heritage, 1998 *Capital archaeology: strategies for sustaining the historic legacy of a world city*, London

Geotechnical Developments (UK) Ltd, 1998 Desk study and phase 1 risk assessment report for land at 165 Rotherhithe Street, London, unpub rep

Goodburn, D, 1982 Wood and woodlands; carpenters and carpentry, in Milne and Milne, 106–31

Goodburn, D, 1991 New light on early ship and boat building in the London area, in *Waterfront archaeology; proc 3rd international conference, Bristol, 1988* (eds G Good, R Jones and M Ponsford), CBA Res Rep 74, 105–11, London

Goodburn, D, 1996 A preliminary assessment of the woodwork found at the Rotherhithe Shafts site (RTH96), unpub MoL rep

Goodburn, D, 1999 Echoes of axes, adzes and pitsaws, in *Old and new worlds* (eds G Egan and R Michael), 171–9, Oxford

Goodburn, D, 2000 A review of recent work on the archaeology of ship and boat building on the Thames, in Rankin (ed), 18–23

Goodburn, D, 2001 The woodworking evidence, in Tyler, 72–7

Goodburn, D, 2002 Analysis of the ship timbers from the south bank excavation, in Ayre and Wroe-Brown, 85–90

Goodburn, D, in prep The woodwork evidence, in Bluer, R and Blatherwick, S, *Medieval moated houses of Southwark: the Rosary, Rotherhithe and Fastolf Place* MoLAS Monogr Ser

Goodburn, D, and Minkin, J, 1999 Woodwork from St Ethelburga's church, City of London (SEH94), unpub MoL rep

Goodburn, D, and Minkin, J, 2000 Details of the carpentry at the Middle Temple Gatehouse, City of London, unpub MoL rep

Goodwin, P, 1987 *The construction and fitting of the sailing man of war 1650–1850*, London

Gover, J E B, Mawer, A, and Stenton, F M, 1934 *The place names of Surrey*, Engl Place Names Soc 11, Cambridge

Haddock, R, 1989 (1684) *A survey of the buildings and encroachments on the river of Thames … / taken by the principal officers and commissioners of his Majesties Navy …*, London, repr St Sampson (Canada)

Horwood, R, 1792–9 *Plan of the Cities of London and Westminster, the borough of Southwark, and parts adjoining showing every house*, London

Horwood, R, 1813 Plan of the Cities of London and Westminster, the borough of Southwark, 3 edn, reproduced in Margary, H, 1985 *The A–Z of Regency London*, Margary in assoc Guildhall Library, Kent

Howe, E, and Seeley, D, 2000 165 Rotherhithe Street, London SE16: project design for an archaeological excavation and watching brief, unpub MoL rep

Humphrey, S, 1997 (1980) *The story of Rotherhithe*, new edn, London Borough of Southwark, Neighbourhood History 6, London

Jamieson, D, 2002 Bombay Wharf, Ceylon Wharf and East India Wharf and 101–105 Rotherhithe Street, London SE16: a report on the evaluation, unpub MoL rep

Jefferies, N, 2000 Assessment report on the post-Roman pottery from 165 Rotherhithe Street, London Borough of Southwark, SE16, unpub MoL rep

Latham, R, 1985 *The shorter Pepys*, Middlesex

Lavery, B, 1991 *Building the wooden walls: the design and construction of the 74-gun ship Valiant*, Greenwich

Lemee, C, 1997 A ship cemetery on the B and W site in Christianshavn, *Maritime Archaeol Newsl from Roskilde*, 29–34

Mackinder, A T, 1998 An archaeological evaluation at 167 Rotherhithe Street, SE16, London Borough of Southwark, unpub MoL rep

Marsden, P, 1996 *Ships of the port of London: 12th to 17th centuries AD*, Engl Heritage Archaeol Rep 5, London

Martin, C J M, 1978 The Dartmouth: a British frigate wrecked off Mull, 1690, *Internat J Naut Archaeol* 7, 29–58

Milne, G, 1992 *Timber building techniques in London, c 900–1400*, London Middlesex Archaeol Soc Spec Pap 15, London

Milne, G, and Milne C, 1982 *Medieval waterfront development at Trig Lane, London*, London Middlesex Archaeol Soc Spec Pap 5, London

MoLAS, 2000 *The archaeology of Greater London: an assessment of archaeological evidence for human presence in the area now covered by Greater London*, London

Morgan, W, 1682 London &c actually surveyed, reproduced in Margary, H, 1977 *London &c actually surveyed by William Morgan, 1682*, Margary in assoc Guildhall Library, Kent

Oertling, T, 1996 *Ships' bilge pumps: a history of their development, 1500–1900*, Texas

Oswald, A, 1975 *Clay pipes for the archaeologist*, BAR Brit Ser 14, Oxford

Pitt, K, and Goodburn, D M, in prep 18th- and 19th-century shipyards: excavations at the south-east entrance to the West India Docks, London, *Internat J Naut Archaeol*

Pullen, J, 1720 A map of the parish of St Mary, Rotherhithe, London, originally engraved by John Harris for the 1720 edn of John Stow, *A survey of London*, London

Rackham, O, 1976 *Trees and woodland in the British landscape*, London

Rankin, S, 1997 *Shipbuilding in Rotherhithe: an historical introduction*, Rotherhithe Local Hist Pap 1, London

Rankin, S, 2000 *Shipbuilding in Rotherhithe: Bull Head Dock to the Pageants*, part 1, Rotherhithe Local Hist Pap 4a, London

Rankin, S (ed), 2000 *Shipbuilding on the Thames and Thames-built ships*, Rotherhithe and Bermondsey Local Hist Group, London

Rocque, J, 1746 A plan of the Cities of London Westminster and Southwark with contiguous buildings from an actual survey by John Rocque, reproduced in Margary, H, 1971 *A plan of the Cities of London Westminster and Southwark by John Rocque, 1746*, Margary in assoc Guildhall Library, Kent

Saxby, D, and Goodburn, D, 1998 17th-century ships' timbers and dock on the Thames waterfront at Bellamy's Wharf, Rotherhithe, London SE16, *Mar Mirror* 84, 173–98

Seeley, D, 2000 Method statement and project design specification for an archaeological evaluation to be carried out at 165 Rotherhithe Street, London SE16, unpub MoL rep

Sidell, J, Cotton, J, Rayner, L, and Wheeler, L, 2002 *The prehistory and topography of Southwark and Lambeth*, MoLAS Monogr Ser 14, London

Southwark Council, 1995 *Unitary development plan*, London

Stammers, M, 1999 Slipways and steamchests: the archaeology of 18th- and 19th-century wooden merchant shipyards in the United Kingdom, *Internat J Naut Archaeol* 28, 253–64

Steel, D, 1794 *The elements and practice of rigging and seamanship, vol 1*, London

Steel, D, 1818 *The art of mast, block and oar making*, London

Steel, D, 1997 (1805) *The elements and practice of naval architecture*, repr, London

Tyers, I, 2000 Dendrochronological spot-dates of samples from Rotherhithe Street (ROZ00) London SE16, unpub MoL rep

Tyler, K, 2001 The excavation of an Elizabethan/Stuart waterfront site on the north bank of the River Thames at Victoria Wharf, Narrow Street, Limehouse, London E14, *Post-Medieval Archaeol* 35, 53–95

Tyler, K, Stephenson, R, and Betts, I, in prep *London's delftware industry: the tin-glazed pottery industries of Southwark and Lambeth*, MoLAS Monogr Ser, London

Upham, N E, 1983 *Anchors*, Shire Album 110, Princes Risborough

Walton Rogers, P, 2002 Cordage and caulking materials from 165 Rotherhithe Street, Southwark, London (ROZ00), unpub Archaeological Textiles Research rep

Watson, B, Brigham, T, and Dyson, T, 2001 *London Bridge: 2000 years of a river crossing,* MoLAS Monogr Ser 8, London

Wilcox, L, A, 1966 Mr *Pepys' navy,* London

Williams, J, and Brown, N (eds), 1999 *An archaeological research framework for the Greater Thames Estuary,* Essex

INDEX

Compiled by Susan Vaughan

Page numbers in **bold** refer to illustrations
B   Building
OA Open Area
S   Structure

Aaron Manby 4
Admiral Rainier 25
Admiralty 4, 8, 24
anchor 27, **30**, 46, 48
Aquilon 19
axe/adze marks 43, 44–5

Baltic, timber from 8, 35
bands, iron 46
Beatson family 24–6, 30, 47
  David 24
  John 24, 25, 26
  William 24
beech 43
Beech, William Phillip 26, 30
Bellamy's Wharf
  excavation 32
  location **2**
  piles 21
  waterfront 15, 34
Bellerophon 25
Bermondsey
  abbey of St Saviour 3
  manor 3
Bermondsey Wall East, excavations 4
Black Cock 9
Blackwall, shipyard 44
bolts, iron 38
bricks 14
Buckingham, HMS **13**
Bucklers Hard (Hants), maritime site 34
Building 1 (privy) **10**, 12, 14, 27
Building 2 (brick building) **10**, 14, 15, 16, 19
Building 3 (timber piles) **20**, 21, 24
Building 4 (John Beatson's house) 25, **25**, 26, **27–9**, 30
Building 5 (warehouse) 25, 26, **27**, **29**, 30, 47
Building 6 (dock-side building) 26–7, **27–9**, 30, 41–6, **43–5**, 47
Bull Head Wharf 24
Bull Head yard/dock 9, 19, 20, 24, 31, 47
  location **2**

Captivity 25
carpentry 32, 34, 48
  anchor 46
  pumps 38–41, **38–41**
  trestle foundation 41–6, **44–5**
  Waterfront 1 34–8, **35–6**
Castle, William 4
cellar 14
cesspit/soakaway (S14) 27
channels, timber-lined *see* Structures 4 and 5
Charles I 8
Charybdis 25
Chatham dockyard 22, 41–2
Christchurch (Southwark), great dock 9
church of St Ethelburga 35
City of London Boys School 34, 36
clay tobacco pipes
  period 2 12, 13, 15
  period 3 18, 19
  period 4 21, 24
Clevely, John the Elder, drawing by 13, **13**, 41

coal 17
Collins, Captain, map by 8, **9**, 13, 15, 16
Collins and Graffingham, Messrs 9
Commercial and Surrey docks 4
crane bases
  period 2 (S3) **10**, 14–15, 16
  period 4 (S11–S13) 22, **23**, 24
  period 5 (S15) 27, 29, **29**, 30, 46
cranes
  documentary evidence 9
  reconstructing 41, **42**

Dartmouth, HMS 37
deal 26
decking *see* Structure 7
dendrochronology
  trestle foundation 14–15
  Waterfront 1 11, 37, 38
Deptford 20
Deptford
  archaeological observations 32
  naval dockyard 12, **13**, 41
  waterfront sheathing 35
Dering, Edward 8
Dinorwic quarry 31
dock-side building *see* Building 6
documentary evidence
  historical background 3–5
  period 2 7–9, **8**, **9**
  period 3 16, **16**
  period 4 **19**, 19–20
  period 5 24–6, **24–6**
  period 6 30–1
Dodd, G, drawing by 44, **45**
Dodds, James 41
dogs, iron 43
drains *see* Structure 2; Structures 8–10; Structure 17
dry dock, documentary evidence
  period 2 9
  period 3 16
  period 4 19, 24
  period 5 24
  period 6 30
dumps
  period 2 11–12, 13, 14
  period 3 17, 18
  period 4 20, 21
Dutch Wars 4, 8–9

East India Company 4, 25
Edward III 4
elm, use of
  anchor 46
  channels 18
  crane bases 22, 27
  pump 14, 40
  shipbuilding 43
  trestle 15
European 8
excavation method 1–2, **3**

Faden, William, map by 25, **25**
Fitzpatrick Construction Ltd 1
flooding 4, 11, 15, 24, 47

garden 16
Garland, HMS 25
geology 6–7, **7**
geotechnical survey 1

Giant Knot Garden 35
Gill, Brian 32
goat hair 37
Gottenburg (Sweden), timber from 8, 16
Gould, Thomas 9, 15
Graffingham *see* Collins and Graffingham
Grampus 24
Grand Surrey Canal 24
great bank of ooze 9, 13, 36
Great Black Cock 8–9
Greenwich Reach 35
groyne *see* Structure 1
Guild of Free Shipwrights 4

Half Moon, public house 8
Half Moon Alley 8
Harvey, Sir Eliab 24
hemp 37
Henry I 3
Henry of Hampton 4
Horwood, Richard, map by 19, **19**, 24
house *see* Building 4
Howland Great Wet Dock 4

James II 8
jetty 14
Jones, Christopher 4
Justitia 25

keels, reused **36**, 37–8
kiln furniture 12, 13, 14, 15
Kitchen 4

land reclamation, medieval 3–4
land-tie beams 48
  period 2 9, **11**, 12, 15, 34–5, **35**
  period 3 16, 17, **18**
  period 4 20, 21
Little Bull's Head Tavern 19
Lloyd, Mr 30
Lothair 4
luting 37

McGhie, Brodie Augustus 24
Mayflower 4
merchants' marks 43
Merlin 8
Middle Temple Gatehouse 35, 36
Millennium footbridge site 34
Monmouth 4
Moore, Sir John 15
Mooring Lighter No. 3 20
Morgan, William, map by 8, **8**, 14, 16
mould, dish 12, **12**; *see also* sugar moulds

nails, iron 9, 17, 35
Navy Board 8, 20
New England, timber from 8, 16

oak, use of
  Building 6 26
  channels 18
  crane bases 22, 27, 29
  drains 14, 21
  privy 12
  pump 40
  shipbuilding 43, 44, 45
  trestle foundation 14, 15
  Waterfront 1 9, 12, 15, 34, 35–6, 37
  Waterfront 3 16, 17
  Waterfront 4 20
  see also treenails
oakum 37
Open Area 2 11–12, 14, 16, 18, 19
Open Area 3 21
Open Area 4 21, **22**
Open Area 5 27
orchard 16
oyster shells 13

Pacific Wharf 1, **2**, 31
paint 14, 22, 37, 43, 46
patches, lead 14
Pepys, Samuel 8, 35

Pier head, Isle of Dogs 34
pine 35–6, 46
Platform Wharf 11
pottery
  period 2 15
    biscuit ware 11–12, **12**, 13, 14, 15
    Dutch slipware 13
    Frechen stoneware 12, 13, **14**
    metropolitan slipware 12
    redware 13, 15
    sugar moulds 13
    tin-glazed ware 12, 15
    Weser slipware 13
  period 3 18, 19
    Lambeth polychrome wares 18
    Staffordshire brown-glazed ware 18
    tin-glazed ware 18, **18**
  period 4 21, 24
    blanche white mug 21, **21**
    Staffordshire buff-bodied fabric 21
  period 5 27, 29
  see also mould
prison ships 25
privy 12, **13**; *see also* Building 1
Pullen, John, map by 8, 16
pump making 34, **38–41**
pumps, reused
  period 2 **11**, 14, **40**
  period 5 **22**, 29, **31**, 40–1, **41**

Queen, HMS 26, **26**

Radcliff, guild 4
Rankin, Stuart 16, 32
'Rederheia' 3
Redriff 3
Regent 4
Rising Star 4
river levels 7, 15, 48
river wall, medieval 3–4
river wall 1
  archaeology 9, **10–11**, 11–13
  carpentry 34–8, **35–6**
  discussion 15, 16, 47
river wall 2
  archaeology **10–11**, 12–14
  discussion 15–16
river wall 3
  archaeology 16–18, **17–18**
  discussion 19
river wall 4
  archaeology 20, **20**
  discussion 24
river wall 5 31
river wall, period 6 30
Rochester 25
Rocque, John, map by 8, 16, **16**, 19
rods, iron 21
Rokesle, Gregory de 3
Rotherhithe
  church of St Mary 3, 4
  manor 3
  pot-house 11, 12
  settlement 3, 4
Rotherhithe shipwrights' charter 4
Rotherhithe Street (Shipwright Street) 4, 8, 14, 25
Rotterdam 24
Royal Navy
  commander 8
  ships built for 4, 5, 19–20, 47
  ships sold by 24, 25, 26

Sailing Lighter No. 2 20
St Ethelburga, church 35
St Mary Church Street, excavation 3, 4
Salisbury 24
saw marks 34, 43
Sesostris 25
shed 25
Sheerness 20
sheet, lead **31**, 41
ship-breakers' yard
  archaeological evidence 27, **27–30**
  discussion 30, 47
  documentary evidence 24–6, **24–6**

ship breaking and repair 4, 5
ship remains, in London area 32, **33**, 34; *see also* ship's timbers, reused
shipbuilding
    history of 4–5
    technology 32–4, 37–8, 42–6, 47
    see also shipyard, period 4
ship's timbers, reused 48
    period 2
        Waterfront 1 9, 11, 12, 15, **36**, 37–8
        Waterfront 2 11, 14
    period 3, Waterfront 3 17, **18**
    period 4
        crane bases 22, **23**
        decking 21
    period 5
        Building 6 27, **36**, 42–6, **44–5**
        crane base 27, **28**, 29
        Structure 16 **28**, 29
        Structure 17 29, **31**
    see also anchor; keels; pumps
Shipwright Street *see* Rotherhithe Street
shipwright's marks 22, **23**, 43
shipyard, period 4
    archaeology **20**, 20–2, **22–3**, 24
    discussion 24, 47
    documentary evidence **19**, 19–20
shipyards, Thames 32, **33**, 34
Shorter family 8, 16, 47
    Charles 8
    Isabella 9
    Sir John 8, 9, 15
    John the younger 8, 9
slag 17, 31
slate 31
'Slede' 3
soakaway *see* cesspit/soakaway
spikes, iron 17, 21, 27, 34, 37
steamships 4
straps, iron 9, 11, 34–5, **35**
strikes, 19th century 5

Structure 1 (groyne) 11, **22**
Structure 2 (drain) **11**, 14, **22**, 40
Structure 3 (trestle foundation) 14–15, 16
Structure 4 (timber-lined channel) **11**, 18, 19
Structure 5 (timber-lined channel) 18, 19
Structure 6 (wet dock) **20**, 20–1, 24, **27**, **29**, 31, 47
Structure 7 (timber decking) **20**, 21
Structures 8–10 (timber drains) **20**, 21, **22**
Structures 11–13 (crane bases) 22, **23**, 24, 41
Structure 14 (cesspit/soakaway) 27
Structure 15 (crane base) 27, **29**, 30, 41, 46
Structure 16 (timber structure) 28–9, 29
Structure 17 (gutter/drain) 29, **29**, 31, 40–1, **41**
sugar moulds 13
Sun Assurance policies 19, 24
Surrey Canal Wharf **24–5**, 24–6, 30
Surrey Commercial Wharf 31
Swinsound 8

Taff Vale Railway 26
Tagus 24
Taunton 4
Temeraire 24, **24**
Texel 24
Thames 25
Thames Bank Ironworks 31
Thames, river
    course of 6, 7
    survey 8, 9, **9**
    see also river levels
tiles 15
timber
    in keels 38

in pump making 40
shortage of 4, 35–6
trees used by shipwrights in 17th century 38
see also carpentry; ship's timbers, reused
timber trade
    17th–18th centuries 4, 8, 15, 16, 35, 47
    19th century 4, 26
timber yard
    period 2
        archaeological evidence 9, **10–14**, 11–15
        discussion 15–16
        documentary evidence 7–9, **8–9**
    period 3 19
topography 6–7, 47
Tower of London, tender 20
Treekronen 24
treenails, oak 35, 37, 43–4, **45**, 46
trestle foundations
    period 2 (S3) 14–15, 16
    period 4 (S11–S13) 22, **23**, 24
    period 5 (B6)
        archaeology 26–7, **28**
        carpentry 41–6, **43–5**
tropical hardwood 29, 41
Turner, J M W 24

Valiant, HMS 44
Victoria Wharf, Limehouse 15, 32, 34, 36
Victory, HMS 43

warehouse *see* Building 5
Warren, Sir William 8, 16, 35, 47
Warren Hastings 25
warships 4
Waterfront 1 47
    archaeology 9, **10–11**, 12–13
    carpentry 34–6, **35–6**
    discussion 15, 16

reused ship timbers **36**, 37–8
    use of 36–7
Waterfront 2
    archaeology **10–11**, 13–14
    discussion 15–16
Waterfront 3
    archaeological evidence 16–18, **17–18**
    discussion 18–19
    documentary evidence 16
Waterfront 4 47
    archaeology 20, **20**
    discussion 24
West India Docks 36, 42
western barge 34
wet dock (S6)
    period 4
        documentary evidence 19
        archaeology **20**, 20–1, 24, 47
    period 5
        documentary evidence 25
        archaeology **27**, 29, **29**
    period 6 31
wharves
    period 2 16, 36, 47
    period 3 17, 19
    period 5 25
    period 6 30–1
William Rufus 3
Wood, William 8
woodworking *see* carpentry
Woolcombe family 24, 47
    Hugh 20
    William 19, 20
    William the younger 20
Woolcombe's Yard 25
Woolwich dockyard 20

yards
    period 2 (OA2) 14, 16
    period 5 (OA5) 27, 47
Young, Josh 19
Young, Hawks and McGhie 24